Bob,

Your life has been special AND GOD continues to bless you!

I hope and pray this book will be another of HIS OTHER WAYS to help spread the gospel message.

Isaiah 55: 8-9

Ken

PS Your stories are on pages 10-15

Miracles, Prophecy and God's Other Ways

How God Works In Today's World

Kenneth Robb Kersey

WestBow
PRESS
A DIVISION OF THOMAS NELSON

Copyright © 2012 by Kenneth Robb Kersey.

All rights reserved. No part of this book may be used or reproduced by any means, graphic, electronic, or mechanical, including photocopying, recording, taping or by any information storage retrieval system without the written permission of the publisher except in the case of brief quotations embodied in critical articles and reviews.

"Scripture quotations taken from the New American Standard Bible®, Copyright© 1960, 1962, 1963, 1968, 1971, 1972, 1973, 1975, 1977, 1995 by The Lockman Foundation. Used by permission." (www.Lockman.org)

WestBow Press books may be ordered through booksellers or by contacting:

WestBow Press
A Division of Thomas Nelson
1663 Liberty Drive
Bloomington, IN 47403
www.westbowpress.com
1-(866) 928-1240

Because of the dynamic nature of the Internet, any web addresses or links contained in this book may have changed since publication and may no longer be valid. The views expressed in this work are solely those of the author and do not necessarily reflect the views of the publisher, and the publisher hereby disclaims any responsibility for them.

Cover Design
Glenn Hadsall
Bottle Rocket
http://www.bottle-rocket.com

Cover Illustration
Mark Ross
Mark Ross Studio
http://www.markrossstudio.com

ISBN: 978-1-4497-4392-5 (hc)
ISBN: 978-1-4497-4393-2 (sc)
ISBN: 978-1-4497-4394-9 (e)

Library of Congress Control Number: 2012905098

Printed in the United States of America

WestBow Press rev. date: 06/11/2012

CONTENTS

Acknowledgements xi

The Beginning xiii

MIRACLES 1

Imprisoned Man Preaches In Iranian Court 3
Crushed by Truck—Angels to the Rescue................................... 6
God Made Her Invisible to Prison Guards 9
God Was the Driver.. 10
Demons Expelled 12
She Saw Heaven and Hell 16
The Man Who Could Not Be Shot... 18
Dead Man Lives to Preach... 22
Missionaries Protected in the South Pacific 24
Angels Guard Missionary in the Middle East 25
Panic to God's Peace in a Flash... 26
God Knows What I Said 28

PROPHECY 31

INCREASE IN TRAVEL AND KNOWLEDGE 35
Communion on the Moon 35
Earth Without Oceans 38
Vertical Farming—New Way to Feed the World 39
Gospel Translated for the World 42
Tweeting for God 44
Finding Oil and Gas In Israel 45
Papyrus to Pixels 50

REACHING NATIONS WITH THE GOSPEL 55

The Gospel Made Known by Bibles 56
Bibles Fall From the Sky! 60
Meeting God Under The Ocean 61
A Grandmother's Last Words—"Don't Wait" 62
From Deep Despair to the Mountaintop 63
Devil Worshiper Becomes A Christian 66
Dad Was Saved Just in Time 70
Hospital Bible Comforts and Saves Two 71
Legacy of a Grandmother's Bible 72
God Changes Taxi Driver's Plans 74
One Bible Saves Forty 74
A Pistol or a Gideon Bible? 75
He Stole a Bible Instead of Money 76
The Book is to Read, Not to Smoke 76
Bank's Error Buys Bibles 77

    I Thought I Was a Christian 78

    Muslim Hotels Finally Welcome Bibles 80

    No One Is Ever Too Bad for God's Love 81

The Gospel Proclaimed By Those "Called to Serve" 85

    A Soldier for Christ 86

    Science and Faith are Allies 92

    God Empowers Those He Calls 97

    Hand Grenade Explodes, Leads to a Ministry 105

    Prophet of Prophecy 107

    He Proved Jesus Is True 110

    Missionaries Slain, Wives Continue Ministry 113

    My Way Was Not God's Way 118

    Servant of God in the Making 121

    Ship Ministry Teaches, Preaches and Saves 125

    Translator of the Bible for Millions 128

    God Wanted Him to be A Policeman 130

    Reaching the Unreachable 133

    God's Word Cannot Be Frozen 136

    Tragedy Leads To Life Mission 138

    Tell It Through Evangelism 141

The Gospel Declared Through Sports 144

    Using His Second Chance 145

    An MVP for Christ 148

    The Phoenix of New Orleans 150

    Par Excellence for Christ 153

    Witnessing With His Eyes 156

The Gospel Expressed Through Music 159
- Faith Survives Life's Tragedies 160
- A Musician Since Childhood 164
- Young Child, Big Voice for the Lord 166
- Christian Songwriters of the Century 168

The Gospel Advanced in the Business World 170
- Chick-Fil-A 171
- Hobby Lobby 173
- Mardel Christian Stores 175
- Interstate Battery System of America 177
- JM Eagle Company 179
- A Mission on the Airwaves 182
- The Tea Lady 184
- Holy Land Experience 186
- DaySpring Cards 189
- Marketplace Chaplains 191

GOD'S OTHER WAYS 193

- POW Sustained by God's **POW**er 195
- She Saved Six Years to Buy a Bible 200
- My Hero 202
- Warned to Escape from Hiroshima 208
- Seize Any Chance to Pray 209
- Plant His Word, He Will Grow It 211
- Trials Strengthen Her Faith 213
- God is Sovereign 218
- God Uses Weather and Nature 221
- Wordless Book and Bracelets 227

"Permit the Children to Come to Me" 230
Polio Makes Therapy Her Life's Work 232
Parachuting the Gospel.. 234
She Met God "In the Garden"... 237
Miners Saved Half Mile Underground... 239
Trust Him, God Knows Best.. 242
Loss Turns to Gain.. 244
Answered Prayer Finds Wife... 246
Silent Witness of The Ground Zero Cross.................................... 248
As It Was in the Days of Noah 250

The End.. 255

Notes... 261

Acknowledgements

To my wife, Donna, who gave me encouragement, feedback, her love and assistance throughout the process of putting this book together.

and

To Ralph and Bill, both of whom submitted stories, read the manuscript, offered ideas and suggestions. I am deeply indebted.

The Beginning

One night about eighteen months ago, as I was getting ready for bed, a thought overwhelmed me. God placed an idea in my mind that I should write a book to tell and convince others about how He works in today's world.

This is the first book I have ever written. Since I retired in the year 2000, I have written several autobiographical memory pieces for my family, but never with the thought of publication.

Now, as I look back over my life, I think God prepared me for producing this book project. I studied journalism in college. My profession was in the travel industry, which afforded me the opportunity to travel to all fifty States and to eighty countries all over the world. My knowledge of other people groups and cultures was greatly expanded.

During these travels I experienced many challenging and memorable circumstances. My job also entailed the writing of sales presentations and descriptive travel brochures. The Lord strengthened me daily in my faith and showed me over and over again how fortunate I was to live and raise my family in the United States.

Even the title of this book, *Miracles . . . Prophecy and God's OTHER WAYS*, with the subtitle *How God Works in Today's World* is His origination, not mine.

The stories you are about to read were gathered after reading thousands of pages and listening to hundreds of radio broadcasts.

Many came from viewing dozens of television programs. Some of the stories were received through personal interviews or by e-mail. Each story actually happened and is documented.

Many of the stories tell about events that are occurring in today's world. They describe personal experiences and are testimonies of people you may have heard of and many you do not know. Some of the events related are miraculous in nature. All of them show how our Sovereign God is at work, and many relate how biblical prophecies about the End Times are being fulfilled.

On many occasions I have gotten up in the night to write down ideas that *popped* into my head. At one point in the book-writing process, I was having extreme difficulty making any progress. Then one night I felt compelled to get up and work on this book.

That night I couldn't write fast enough. More progress was made that night than I had made in a month.

For the past few months, I have wondered how the book should be distributed. I kept coming to the same answer, that He wants it distributed as widely as possible. As a result, it is available in both print and electronically.

I have no idea just how God plans to use this book, but I know His hand has been directing its creation. I hope and pray it will be another of His OTHER WAYS to spread the Good News about God's gift of our salvation.

MIRACLES

MIRACLES HAPPEN EVERY DAY!!

We often take miracles, such as the rising of the morning sun or a small flower opening its bloom, for granted. Maybe we take for granted salmon travelling thousands of miles and navigating dozens of streams to return to their birthplace in order to spawn new salmon. We also marvel when bees swarm in harmony, flocks of birds fly in unison, or schools of fish swim in perfect precision. These are miracles of God's creation.

In his book *Miracles*[1], C. S. Lewis takes nearly three hundred pages to define the word *miracle*. For the purpose of this book, we shall define a miracle as an event that cannot be duplicated by man and is impossible without God's intervention. A good friend calls such an event a "Grade A" miracle.

Jesus performed many "Grade A" miracles while He was on earth, thirty-six of which are recorded in the New Testament. Among them are miracles concerning nature, demonic power, physical healing, and the supplying of physical needs. Some of these are described in the following New Testament passages:

Calmed the turbulent sea	Mark 4:35-40
Turned water into wine	John 2:1-11
Raised Lazarus from the dead	John 11:43, 44

Walked on water	Matthew 14:22-33
Expelled demons	Matt. 8:28-34, Mark 5:1-20, Luke 8:26-39
Healed the cripple at Bethesda	John 5:1-15
Restored sight to the blind	Matthew 9:27-31, 20:30-34, Mark 8:22-26, John 9:1-7
Fed the 5,000	Matthew 14:15-21

In addition to these miracles, the account of His own miraculous resurrection from the dead is recorded in all four Gospels: Matthew 28, Mark 16, Luke 24, and John 20.

God continues to perform miracles. Believers in Jesus Christ consider miraculous things that happened to them to be true miracles and believe God intervened to make them happen. Atheists, agnostics and other non-believers in God often consider such events to be mere accidents or extreme coincidences and try to explain them away. However, those involved are convinced the event in their own life was a miracle.

The stories that follow tell of incredible events that have happened to people in recent times as contrasted to those recorded in biblical times. Most of these accounts are told about individuals who are still living. God's love and intervening power are demonstrated in these stories. The events that occurred cannot be easily explained away—they really happened. There are thousands of such stories. Here are just a few of them.

As you read this book, I suggest you have a Bible handy to look up some of the Bible references.

IMPRISONED MAN PREACHES IN IRANIAN COURT

Dan Baumann spent many years as a Christian missionary in Muslim countries. It was a very dangerous undertaking. In January of 1997 he and a fellow missionary began a two-week visit to Iran. While they were there they came to love the country and its people. All was fine until they prepared to leave Iran and return to the United States.

After turning in their travel documents to be stamped, they were detained at the border exit. They were told there was a problem with their papers. The two men were separated and put in separate rooms where they were beaten and interrogated for the next six hours. Then they were dressed in prison clothes, blindfolded and put in separate cells. Dan and his friend were imprisoned in Iran! There was nothing they could do. They would have to rely on God to perform a miracle to rescue them from their situation.

In his isolated cell it was hard for Dan to sense any feeling of God. All he could do was trust the Lord and know that He was true no matter how Dan felt or what his captors did to him. His cell had only one dim light in a corner, and it was on twenty-four hours a day. It was wintertime and the heater in the cell did not work well. He only left the cell when he was taken each day into a dark interrogation room with blood-stained floors. There he was beaten, slapped, punched and kicked. It was a terrifying experience.

There came a time when Dan doubted he could go on, and he resolved to end his life. He tried four times to drown himself in a small sink in the cell, but each time he was too afraid to carry it through. He was completely broken in spirit and felt great shame.

One day, all of a sudden, the cell was filled with a bright light, and there was Jesus saying to him, "Dan, I love you, and I promise to carry you through this time."[1] From that moment on Dan never had those doubting thoughts again.

His encounter with Jesus challenged his attitude towards his interrogator. He was able to see him as God saw and loved him. At the next interrogation, Dan found himself telling the interrogator that if they were going to continue to meet, they should become friends and call one another by name.

At first the interrogator refused, but then Dan stuck out his hand. The man froze and after a few minutes began to visibly shake. Slowly, he extended his hand to Dan and tears started rolling down his cheeks. He looked at Dan, told Dan his name and said he would also like to be his friend. There is no heart that is too hard for Jesus to soften. He had taught Dan to love his enemy.

Later Dan overheard some of the guards talking about him and his friend, how they were Christians and followers of Jesus. The guards had seen how Dan had a reason to live and a reason to die, and they wanted that, too. They wanted to know Jesus and learn about His ways. Dan now knew why he had been put in the prison.

Dan was placed under two death sentences, one as a missionary and one as a spy. When it was his time to appear in court before the judge, along with cameras and hundreds of people, he was asked why he had come to Iran.

Dan felt the power of the Lord surge in him. He looked directly at the judge and said, "I came to Iran to tell you about

Jesus Christ."[2] He said it again and again, and then for the next twenty minutes preached the Gospel and told the people in the courtroom how God loved them. Dan knew he was free no matter what happened to him on earth—he had a home in Heaven with Jesus. No one could take that away from him. Dan was imprisoned for nine weeks in Iran, and then released by the country's highest court. He received the miracle he had hoped for.

Today Dan serves with Youth With a Mission at YWAM headquarters in Trinidad, Colorado. He has written two books, *Imprisoned in Iran—Love's Victory Over Fear*, and *A Beautiful Way*.

CRUSHED BY TRUCK—
ANGELS TO THE RESCUE

Bruce Van Natta was a self-employed diesel mechanic who loved his work. He was never concerned about the danger he risked working on huge engines weighing thousands of pounds. Then, on November 16, 2006, his life changed forever.

This is Bruce Van Natta's story.

Bruce had a job to work on the engine of a huge PeterBilt logging truck. The driver of the truck had jacked up the front axle and had removed the passenger side wheel. Without giving it a second thought Bruce slipped feet first underneath the large bumper of the vehicle. Bruce's chest was positioned just an inch or two below the axle. He asked the driver to look inside the truck to check the temperature of the engine. All of a sudden, the twenty-ton capacity jack that was holding up the truck gave way.

There were some 10,000 to 12,000 pounds of weight from the wheels and axle that fell on Bruce's mid-section. It literally crushed him in half as blood splattered into his throat. Bruce realized there was no more than an inch from the bottom of the axle to the cement, and the thickest part of his body was no more than two inches thick. Vertebrae were broken by the crushing weight of the truck.

Though he experienced absolutely horrendous pain, he was able to pull himself a short distance so that his head was in front of the bumper. Bruce called out to God twice asking for His help. Suddenly all pain left Bruce's body. He became unconscious. His spirit left his body, and he was looking down at the scene of the accident from above.[1]

At this point, Bruce saw two huge angels. Each was about eight feet tall, and they were surrounded in bright light. They never moved or said anything; they just angled their arms towards his body. Bruce felt no pain, just a wonderful peace.

Bruce realized he had to make a choice. He could just shut his eyes, die, and go to Heaven, or he could fight to live, fight as hard as he could. Bruce says, "The next thing I knew, my spirit went back down into my body just like a shot."[2]

Bruce was rushed to the hospital, where doctors did not expect him to live. His ribs were broken, his pancreas, spleen, and intestines crushed. Several major arteries were severed.

A medical study done at the University of Southern California in 2001 could not find anyone who had ever lived after having five major arteries severed. It was amazing that Bruce had not bled to death. He believes that the angels miraculously held him together.[3]

Bruce was in the hospital for over two months and had five major surgeries that resulted in the removal of almost seventy-five percent of his crushed small intestines. He dropped weight rapidly and was close to starvation. He could be fed only through intravenous tubes.

One day he had an unexpected visitor. The Lord had awakened a man from New York two days in a row with the urging to go to see Bruce in the hospital and pray for his healing. The man was someone Bruce had met one time on vacation. When he got to the hospital, he put his palm on Bruce's forehead. Then the man prayed in the name of Jesus commanding Bruce's intestines to be restored in length. Bruce says, "When he did, I felt like two hundred twenty volts come out of his palm into my forehead, right into my body. I could feel my intestines moving around and up and down."[4]

Nine months later, after additional surgeries and hospital stays, Bruce had gained weight and was eating by himself. Radiology tests verified that he now had almost nine feet of small intestine—double the amount that he had had after the first surgeries. Additionally, his intestines had double the absorption action of normal intestines.[5]

The doctors were amazed and astounded over and over again that Bruce lived through this trauma. He should have died within eight to ten minutes after the accident. Bruce could have bled to death, but didn't. His intestines grew back, and they were extended and better functioning than before. His pancreas and spleen were restored. Bruce strongly believes that God performed these miracles in his life.

Bruce wrote about his experience in a book called *Saved By Angels to Share How God Talks to Everyday People*, published by Destiny Image. He has a full-time ministry with a non-denominational, evangelistic organization called SweetBread Ministries.

He and his family travel together witnessing to gatherings of people about how God worked in his life to heal him and how others can also have a closer relationship with the Lord. Their testimony shows how God's love and power meet each of us at our point of need. Read more at Bruce's website: www.sweetbreadministries.com/.

GOD MADE HER INVISIBLE TO PRISON GUARDS

The following story is told by Corrie ten Boom in her book *A Prisoner and Yet*. It is similar to the story in Acts 12 when Peter was in prison and an angel helped him walk past guards and escape. The guards didn't see him.

During World War II Corrie ten Boom and her sister Betsie arrived at one of the Nazi concentration camps. All new prisoners were being searched for any type of contraband. Corrie had a Bible she wanted to keep, so she hid it under her dress.

She says, "it did bulge out obviously through my dress; but I prayed, 'Lord, cause now Thine angels to surround me; and let them not be transparent today, for the guards must not see me.' I felt perfectly at ease. Calmly I passed the guards. Everyone was checked, from the front, the sides, and the back. Not a bulge escaped the eyes of the guard. The woman just in front of me had hidden a woolen vest under her dress; it was taken from her. They let me pass, for they did not see me. Betsie, right behind me, was searched."[1]

A second group of guards searched them, but again Corrie was not seen. She writes, "I knew they would not see me, for the angels were still surrounding me. I was not even surprised when they passed me by; but within me rose the jubilant cry, 'O Lord, if Thou dost so answer prayer, I can face even Ravensbruck unafraid.'"[2]

(Ravensbruck was a concentration camp for female German prisoners in World War II.)

GOD WAS THE DRIVER

Bob Christopher is my good friend from church. He offered to share this story. It is a testimony of how God supernaturally intervened to protect his daughter, Karen, and her family from instant disaster. Following is her e-mail account of the incident.

"We were leaving the Georgia Dome in Atlanta traveling north in the fast lane (left lane) of Georgia State Highway 400 at about seventy miles per hour in heavy traffic. My husband started coughing and asked me to take the wheel, because he was getting dizzy. We started to move to the right, so I thought he was pulling over. Then I looked over at him and realized that he had passed out. When I looked back to the right, we were on one of the long straight exits off of Highway 400. I only had to straighten the wheel slightly to keep us on the road while I attempted to wake up my husband, Larry.

"I have no idea how we got from the far left lane into the exit (far right lane) without hitting any of the cars that were surrounding us, other than through divine intervention. No one even honked at us, and no tires squealed. If we had veered right one hundred feet sooner, we would have hit the supports for the overpass; one hundred feet later the exit was circular, and I couldn't have negotiated the turn.

"I told my dad that the only logical explanation was that God had supernaturally transported us from the left lane of traffic and placed us on the exit lane with a quarter mile straight lane. This allowed me time to wake up my husband, and he was able to put on the brake just as we approached the intersection."[1]

"Our God moves in a mysterious way His wonders to perform" are the first two lines of a hymn written by William Cowper

(1731-1800). Many events that happen in people's lives are not explainable in human terms. Our Lord is the designer and creator of everything and is in control of all that happens. He is all-knowing and all-powerful. We may not be able to understand the how and why of events now, but someday we will. Jesus said, *"What I do you do not realize now, but you will understand hereafter"* (John 13:7).

We just need to believe in Him and know that He has a plan for each of us and for the world. *"For now we see in a mirror dimly, but then face to face; now I know in part, but then I will know fully just as I also have been fully known"* (I Corinthians 13:12).

DEMONS EXPELLED

Exorcism is commonly known as driving demons out of a demon-possessed person. Many people do not believe in demons or exorcisms. They are skeptical and wary of them. Yet, Jesus was not shy or timid about evicting evil spirits. He personally performed a number of exorcisms, as related in the New Testament.

One of the most well-known reports of Christ performing an exorcism is found in Matthew 8:28-32, which states:

> *"When He came to the other side into the country of the Gadarenes, two men who were demon-possessed met Him as they were coming out of the tombs. They were so extremely violent that no one could pass by that way. And they cried out, saying, 'What business do we have with each other, Son of God? Have You come here to torment us before the time?' Now there was a herd of many swine feeding at a distance from them. The demons began to entreat Him, saying, 'If You are going to cast us out, send us into the herd of swine.' And He said to them, 'Go!' And they came out and went into the swine, and the whole herd rushed down the steep bank into the sea and perished in the waters."*

This same story is also told in Mark 5:1-20 and in Luke 8:26-39. Other occasions when Jesus removed demons are found in Mark 1:21-18 and Luke 4:31-37. Jesus performed at least seven exorcisms that we know about.

Jesus also gave the power of exorcism to seventy of His disciples. He bestowed this power and other powers on them and *"sent them in pairs ahead of Him to every city and place where He Himself was going to come"* (Luke 10:1).

When they came together again, the disciples reported to Jesus saying, *"Lord, even the demons are subject to us in Your name"* (Luke 10:17). Jesus answered, *"Behold, I have given you authority to tread on serpents and scorpions, and over all the power of the enemy, and nothing will injure you"* (Luke 10:19).

My good friend Bob Christopher told me about his experiences with exorcism. Bob was the pastor of various churches in North Carolina from 1981 to 2001. After he retired, he and his wife moved to Texas to be closer to their children and grandchildren. My wife and I became friends with them when they joined our church and fellowship class.

In 1988 Bob began taking numerous short-term mission trips to many areas of the world. Though now retired, he is by no means *completely* retired. To date he has taken more than forty-four mission trips to all parts of the world. The trips were arranged by the International Commission, an evangelistic and discipleship ministry based in Lewisville, Texas. The Commission has a working relationship with the Foreign Mission Board of the Baptist Church.

Bob has witnessed several exorcisms of demons first-hand. He told me about three occasions he observed demon-possessed people during some of these mission trips. The exorcisms took place thousands of miles apart on separate continents and over the space of fifteen years.

The first occasion took place in 1989 in Santiago, Chile. He was preaching at the Argamedo Baptist Church. A lady in the congregation was continually interrupting him and disrupting his preaching. According to Bob, she was a constant "chatterbox". He continued to preach, and eventually the deacons of the church took her to another room and exorcised five demons from her.

Each time a demon came out of her, she screamed. Later that evening, the lady was in her right mind and sane (similar to the story told in Mark 5:15). Bob described her as "sweet". She told of being freed from the demons, about her love for Jesus, and asked for the congregation's forgiveness.

Another occasion took place in Xai Xai (pronounced Shy Shy), Mozambique in 1990 at the Xai Xai Church. A young lady about thirty-five years old said that her demon was about to show itself. Then she went into what he describes as a trance. Bob watched her as she tucked her head to her chest, looking first down, then to the side and up at the ceiling and then again to the other side. She repeated the process for five to ten minutes. Bob didn't see a demonic spirit, but he viewed the actions of the lady and heard the demon speak.

Bob witnessed another exorcism in Lusaka, Zambia, in 2001 at the Missi Baptist Church. While Bob was preaching, a young woman about eighteen years old who practiced witchcraft, went into a trance and began to slither on her side like a snake across the floor. Bob said he did not know how she propelled herself, but her body moved just like a snake. It took the deacons two days of continual praying to complete this exorcism. Some deacons would pray for a few hours, and then other deacons would take over. Finally, the evil spirit was exorcised. Relief came to the lady, but only after the two days of prayer.

This exorcism is similar to the event related in the book of Mark when Jesus performed an exorcism that the disciples were not able to accomplish. The disciples came to Jesus privately and asked "*Why could we not drive it out?*" And Jesus said to them, "*This kind cannot come out by anything but prayer*" (Mark 9:28-29).

Many in the medical profession explain such conditions as being caused by a physical or mental illness. However, cures for physical or mental illnesses take long periods of time. The exorcisms described above are similar to those that Jesus performed because they caused an immediate change in the troubled person.

SHE SAW HEAVEN AND HELL

In her book, *Delivered*,[1] Tamara Laroux tells a story of despair, her suicide attempt and then how she received saving redemption.

Tamara was just six years old when her parents divorced. She was overwhelmed with feelings of rejection, felt completely alone and was in a deep depression—her world just fell apart.

As she grew up, she turned the slightest negative comment or event into a big problem, making a mountain out of molehill. She just could not be happy. She felt if she couldn't be happy, the only answer was to take her own life.[2]

In 1982, when she was fifteen years old, Tamara took a gun from her mother's room and stepped into a shower. She knelt down, put the gun to her temple and asked the Lord to forgive her. Something told her to move the gun from her head and point it at her chest. She placed the gun on her chest to the left side of her heart and pulled the trigger.[3]

Her lungs became filled with blood and she couldn't hear anything. Even though her eyes were open, things went black. She felt her soul leave her body and was no longer in control of anything.

She *fell* into a place that was absolute torment. Like the rich man who died and went to hell in the story Jesus told in Luke 16, she felt her body burning and in excruciating pain. She was tormented by fear and was profoundly lonely and depressed. Others around her were formless beings yelling and crying out in pain. They were begging for a second chance, screaming that people still living on earth should claim Jesus Christ as Lord so they would never come to this place.

Tamara saw the hand of God literally scoop her up and carry her to show her heaven. No longer was she tormented; she felt healed and whole. She experienced the presence of Jesus. "The glory there is too exquisite for words,"[4] says Tamara. She relates that all was so bright and beautiful. She had an astounding feeling of peace and total tranquility and an overwhelming presence of God's love and forgiveness. She was given a strong spiritual strength that she had never before experienced and felt ready to confront what was ahead of her. Then she saw herself returning home and back into her body, and opened her eyes.

The bullet had just missed her heart, and the pressure of the bullet should have exploded it. The doctors were amazed that all she came away with was a few broken ribs.

Tamara now feels joy and peace and knows that God loves her. She has been adopted into God's family. She accepts what He offers as hers to receive. She says, "I have to be able to recognize and replace my junk with His greatness."[5] She knows that she can face anything in life as long as she relies on God's promises and accepts His love and gift of salvation. She now faces life and its problems with strength and a peaceful joy. Tamara concludes, "I can come out on the other side full of hope and a victory in Christ."[6]

Eternity is real. Hell is real. Heaven is real. To get to heaven, you must accept Jesus as Lord, acknowledge He died for your sins and repent, and accept His gift of salvation. The condemned creatures in Hell cried out to those back on earth that they should learn and know the truth. All who leave this earth will either go to a place of eternal torment or to a place of eternal light, love and joy. It is each person's responsibility and decision to decide which route he or she will take.

Miracles, Prophecy and God's Other Ways

THE MAN WHO COULD NOT BE SHOT

David Barton has written the following amazing story found in his book, *The Bulletproof George Washington*. Barton says that at one time, this story of God's divine protection of George Washington could be found in virtually all school textbooks. Now few Americans have read the story or know anything about it, because it is not found in today's textbooks.

This story displays how God works in our world. Without God's intervention George Washington might never have lived to be the "Father of our Country". Washington often told others about this life-changing event that influenced the man he became and affirmed God's plan for his life.

George Washington began his military career in 1754 when he was in his early twenties. He began not as a private but as a major in the militia of Virginia and was promoted to Colonel. At that time, the British colonists had settled the eastern seaboard and claimed all lands in the West. The French settled in Canada and in Louisiana and also claimed land in the West. This created a conflict between the British and the French and resulted in the French and Indian War.

The French made plans to build a series of forts on the Ohio and Mississippi Rivers, stretching from Canada to New Orleans. This action would block the British Colonies from access to the West and make it possible for the French to colonize the area.

Governor Dinwiddie of Virginia commissioned George Washington as an ambassador and sent him with a letter to the French telling them to cease their plans. Washington met the French at Fort Duquesne, which later was renamed Fort Pitt.

(It is now the site of Pittsburgh, Pennsylvania.) Washington was unsuccessful in his efforts, and the French pushed ahead with building the forts.

To protect their interests, the British sent approximately one thousand battle-hardened troops to Virginia and put British General Braddock in charge. Braddock wanted the help of the colonists, so he appointed George Washington as his chief aide and honored his rank of Colonel. Virginia provided another three hundred troops, making a total of thirteen hundred men under Braddock's command. With the help of Benjamin Franklin money, horses, wagons, cannons and supplies were assembled. Braddock and Washington led the troops and trekked several hundred miles through the forests. They built roads as they proceeded to Fort Duquesne.

Braddock was used to the out-in-the-open style of warfare waged in Europe. Washington warned him that the Indians (allies of the French) fought ambush style and shielded themselves behind trees. Braddock wouldn't listen. Twice he refused to believe this same warning from Indians who were friendly to the British. He was so rude to them that they gave up trying to make him understand.

So, Braddock's army stood in their bright red British uniforms, shoulder-to-shoulder, out in the open, completely exposed to the enemy. They were sitting ducks when shots were leveled at them from the forest. The French and Indians suffered only minimal casualties, but the general's army suffered near annihilation. Braddock was killed. It was a slaughter.

The hostile Indian marksmen continued to shoot at the mounted British officers and singled out Washington as a target. "Quick, let your aim be certain and he dies," the chief commanded.[1]

Miracles, Prophecy and God's Other Ways

The warriors aimed their rifles at George Washington on horseback and shot round after round at him. Washington remained unhurt.

The native warriors stared at the scene in disbelief. Their rifles seldom missed their mark. The chief suddenly realized that a mighty power must be shielding this man and told his warriors to stop firing.

As the firing slowed, Washington gathered the few remaining troops and led the retreat to safety. That evening, as the last of the wounded were being cared for, Washington noticed an odd tear in his coat. It was a bullet hole! He rolled up his sleeve and looked at his arm directly under the hole. There was no mark on his skin. Amazed, he took off his coat and found three more holes where bullets had passed through his coat but stopped before they reached his body.

Nine days after the battle, after hearing the rumor circulating about his death, Washington wrote his brother John to confirm that he was still very much alive.

"As I have heard since my arrival at this place, a circumstantial account of my death and dying speech, I take this early opportunity of contradicting the first and of assuring you that I have not as yet composed the latter. But by the all-powerful dispensations of Providence I have been protected beyond all human probability or expectation; for I had four bullets through my coat, and two horses shot under me yet escaped unhurt, although death was leveling my companions on every side of me!"[2]

The events that occurred around Colonel Washington that day during the battle provide compelling proof that he was in God's care and survived due to the Lord's direct intervention on his behalf. One of the Indian warriors, who had been a leader in the battle was heard later to relate the events of that day. "Washington was never born to be killed by a bullet! I had seventeen fair fires at him with my rifle, and after all could not bring him to the ground!"[3]

He said, "Listen! The Great Spirit protects that man (indicating Washington), and guides his destinies—he will become the chief of nations, and a people yet unborn will hail him as the founder of a mighty empire. I am come to pay homage to the man who is the particular favorite of Heaven, and who can never die in battle."[4]

George Washington not only survived this battle in 1755, but was not even wounded. He fought other battles as well in his lifetime, but was never wounded in any of them.

"A thousand may fall at your side and ten thousand at your right hand, but it shall not approach you" (Psalm 91:7).

DEAD MAN LIVES TO PREACH

Another story about heaven is one that Don Piper tells in his book *90 Minutes In Heaven*.[1] The book describes events surrounding the time that Don Piper, a pastor, attended the annual Baptist General Convention of Texas held in Houston.

Piper lived in Houston and was driving home from the conference when he was in a horrible car wreck. An eighteen-wheeler struck his red Ford Escort head on. He was killed instantly. Four sets of EMTs declared him dead at the scene. To prevent onlookers from staring at Piper's bloody and mangled body, he was covered with a tarp.

As Don tells the story, he died and went to heaven. While in heaven, Don was greeted by many who had died years before and who were glad to welcome him. He felt inexpressible joy and peace. While there he heard constant music and praises to the Lord. Many different songs played simultaneously, but all were in harmony. Don describes everything as extremely beautiful.

Don relates in his book that another pastor, who had attended the same conference, came upon the accident scene. He didn't know it was Don Piper in the wrecked car. Yet, he felt strangely compelled to stop and to go to the man in the red car, put his hand under the tarp and onto the severely disfigured body, and pray for the dead person lying there. "I felt compelled to pray. I didn't know who the man was or whether he was a believer. I only know that God told me I had to pray for him."[2] The pastor prayed and sang, *What a Friend We Have in Jesus*. It was ninety minutes after the car wreck and after the police and the paramedics had pronounced him dead that Don says, "I began to sing with him."[3]

God performed a miracle that day. Don returned back to life with a broken body. To date he has had thirty-four surgical procedures. The fact that he can walk is a miracle it itself and unexplainable in medical terms. The experience he had in heaven gave him a unique view of eternity and has given him a mission to tell others about Jesus Christ. He empathizes with those who are hurt, discouraged and health-challenged, as he is someone who has been there. His life's work and goal is to minister to people who are bitter and defeated and turn them to the Lord with a guarantee of eternity.

Besides working in full-time Christian ministry since 1984, Don Piper has written many books in addition to *90 Minutes in Heaven*. This book has sold more than 2.7 million copies in the United States. He speaks in pulpits around the world and is also involved with broadcast and media presentations to spread the Word.

Missionaries Protected in the South Pacific

In his book *Angels,* Billy Graham relates the story told by Reverend John G. Paton, a trail-blazing missionary in the South Pacific in the New Hebrides Islands.[1] The story illustrates how God provides angels to protect and care for His believers.

One night Paton and his wife found themselves threatened by hostile natives who surrounded their mission headquarters. The Patons thought for sure that the natives would burn down the headquarters and kill them both. They prayed throughout the night asking God to protect them from harm. The next morning they were astonished when they realized that the natives had gone away. They had no idea where or why they had left. The missionaries again prayed and thanked the Lord for saving them.

About a year later, the chief of the native tribe who had threatened them became a Christian. He came to visit the Patons. When he was asked about the incident of that night of terror, the chief told the Patons that he and his men were too fearful to carry out their plans of attack. They had seen an army of giant men in "shining garments with drawn swords in their hands"[2] surrounding the mission grounds. Paton and the chief agreed that there was no explanation other than that God had sent angels to keep the missionaries from harm.

This story is similar to the one told in 2 Kings 6:17: *"Then Elisha prayed and said, 'O LORD, I pray, open his eyes that he may see.' And the LORD opened the servant's eyes and he saw; and behold, the mountain was full of horses and chariots of fire all around Elisha."*

ANGELS GUARD MISSIONARY IN THE MIDDLE EAST

This story was told to my fellowship class at my church by a missionary our class helps to support. He is truly committed to his mission of spreading God's word to non-believers. The area he travels to is so dangerous, that his real name cannot be given to protect his identity.

Once when he was flying over the Middle East going to his assignment, his flight entered airspace that covered several countries, including his destination. He describes the feeling he had as he entered that air space as "though he was entering a bubble of darkness". Fear gripped him and remained with him for the next several hours.

When he landed, he went to a friend's house. The fear continued! Later as he left the friend's house, he walked down an alley. He thought someone might be following him, so he looked over his shoulder. Behind him he could see several tall guards. He believes these may have been angels sent to protect him.

He was no longer afraid!

Just like Elisha's servant, he was allowed to see God's protection for him. (2 Kings 6:17)

Panic to God's Peace in a Flash

The author of this book, Kenneth Kersey, shares this story.

My wife, Donna and I were living in Cedar Rapids, Iowa. I worked for a large travel corporation that had travel agencies located in Nebraska, Missouri, Illinois and Iowa. As one of the vice presidents, I was responsible for the offices in Iowa and Illinois.

One night around 2:00 a.m. our home telephone rang. It was my boss from Omaha. He told me that the charter flight for Iowa State fans traveling to the Peach Bowl football game in Atlanta was snowed in and still on the ground in Des Moines. It had been scheduled to depart at 11:00 p.m. This was a very special event for Iowa State, and there would be many disappointed fans if they didn't make it to Atlanta in time for the start of the game. The weather reports for Des Moines were not good.

My boss said that he didn't think that the flight would be able to take off and get to Atlanta in time for the kick off. He thought it would be best to have an officer of the company at the airport in Des Moines to break the news. So, he needed me there.

I dressed quickly and started driving the one hundred plus miles to Des Moines. When I first started out the weather was not too bad, and I was able to drive about seventy miles per hour on Interstate 80 that goes from Cedar Rapids to Des Moines.

Then snow began to fall. Ice followed and began to accumulate on the highway. I was getting nervous and my palms began to sweat. I slowed down to about thirty miles per hour. Big semi-trucks were passing me, throwing ice and snow on my windshield.

I drove slower and slower and soon was just creeping along at fifteen to twenty miles per hour. By this time I was tightly gripping the steering-wheel and had to lean forward in the seat to be able to see. The windshield wipers were going as fast as they could go. Then I realized that at my current speed, I would never make it. By the time I would get to the airport, it would be too late. The charter flight would not make it to Atlanta in time for the kickoff. I was worrying and fretting, praying and pleading with the Lord for help.

Then suddenly, a strong sense of peace captured my being. It wasn't like I heard a voice, but more like a thought that came to me that God put in my mind. I just pulled off the road, telephoned my boss and told him, "Everything will be fine. The charter **will** take off in time."

Philippians 4: 6-7 says *"Be anxious for nothing, but in everything by prayer and supplication with thanksgiving let your requests be made known to God. And the peace of God, which surpasses all comprehension, will guard your hearts and your minds in Christ Jesus."*

I experienced that peace. It was a peace I had never felt before. It was the peace of God! As it turned out, the flight did take off at the very last minute that it could and still make it to the game on time

When the plane landed in Atlanta, buses met the group and were escorted by motorcycles directly to the stadium. The Iowa State fans took their seats just seconds before the kickoff. The Lord was in control like He had let me know He would be!

As I look back over the years, I know that God has always been there working in my life. I do not know what He may have in store for my future, but I am content knowing He is in charge.

"Trust in the LORD with all your heart and do not rely on your own understanding. In all your ways acknowledge Him, and He will make your paths straight" (Proverbs 3:5-6).

God Knows What I Said

The author of this book also shares this story.

It was during my sophomore year in high school when I first spoke in tongues. I had no experience like the apostle Paul did when he was on the road to Damascus. There were no bells or whistles. There was no lightning bolt. And there was no rushing wind (Acts 2:2) to signify the occasion. But, as I look back now, God has been working in my life since I was a small boy.

When I was nine years old I became a Christian and gave my life to Jesus Christ. It took place on the playground of the high school that was about two blocks from my house in the Oak Cliff area of Dallas. I had just finished third grade in May, 1948, and I was attending a Vacation Bible School held at the playground that June. About twenty of us children sat on moveable bleachers. There we listened to the VBS teacher, who was about twenty years old, tell us the Gospel story and encourage us to ask Jesus into our hearts.

I have always regretted that I didn't get her name and didn't thank her for leading me to Christ. Becoming a Christian was the most significant experience in my entire life. It is impossible to tell you how my life has been affected by that decision.

I wasn't baptized right away, because shortly after that event my dad was transferred by his employer, the Burlington Railroad (now the BNSF), to Portland, Oregon. There I attended fourth grade. Dad was transferred again in early 1951, this time to the Chicago area. We lived in Aurora, where I attended fifth grade through high school. I was baptized at the First Baptist Church in Aurora. On a trip to the Middle East with my dad, the pastor and the pastor's son in the summer of 1960, I was baptized again—this time in the Jordan River!

Just before entering high school I traveled by train to visit my aunt, uncle and cousins in Towanda, Pennsylvania. While in Towanda, I went with my Aunt Margie and my cousin Katie to their church. I was sitting in the second row from the back of the church. The pastor gave a sermon about speaking in tongues. During the service he asked those who wanted to receive the gift of tongues to come down to the front of the sanctuary.

Trying not to be seen, I slid down in my seat. I still remember what I was wearing—a black suit and my dad's red knit tie. After a few minutes several people had gone down to the front. Then the pastor pointed directly at me, saying, "You in the red tie, come down front." I went down front. There I was, along with perhaps a dozen or so others.

The pastor prayed for all of us to receive the gift of speaking in tongues. We did. It was one of the most spiritually uplifting things that ever happened to me. I have been asked many times what I was saying. My answer is that I don't know. My sense is that the language could not be understood by man. The prayer was private and only God could understand it.

On the ride home from church my cousin Katie and I sat in the back seat. I was still so filled with the Holy Spirit, that I said, "It's hard for me to speak in English". The ability to speak in tongues remained with me until I left Towanda to return home.

Twice since that time I have been praying in normal English but suddenly have spoken in tongues. Both times I was by myself and both times were more than thirty years after my Towanda experience. Once I was at home when I lived in Cedar Rapids, Iowa, and the other when I was driving alone to Aurora, Illinois, to see my dad, who was very ill.

At Pentecost the apostles were all filled with the Holy Spirit and began to speak in other tongues, as the Holy Spirit *"was giving them utterance"*(Acts 2:4). The crowd was amazed and bewildered, as each heard the message in his own language. As is written in Acts 2: 8-11, *"And how is it that we each hear them in our own language to which we were born? . . . we hear them in our own tongues speaking of the mighty deeds of God."*

PROPHECY

The following is found in Josh McDowell's book, *More Than a Carpenter*. It helps explain how Jesus Christ has an address in history, an address that identifies Him for who He was and is for all time; an address proving He was connected to a certain country, a specific race of people, and a town that is identified as His.

> "In the Old Testament there are sixty major messianic prophecies and approximately 270 ramifications that were fulfilled in one person, Jesus Christ. . . . God wrote an 'address' in history to single out His Son, the Messiah, the Savior of mankind, from anyone who has ever lived in history . . ."[1]

The chance of one person fulfilling all of these prophecies is mathematically impossible. Only God was able to make it happen through His Son, Jesus Christ.

Below is a partial listing of the messianic prophecies, the location in the Old Testament and how they were fulfilled as recorded in the New Testament.[2]

Prophecy	**Old Testament**	**New Testament**
Christ's pre-existence	Micah 5:2	Colossians 1:17

Heir to the throne of David	Isaiah 9:7 Jeremiah 23:5	Luke 1:32-33
Born in Bethlehem	Micah 5:2	Matthew 2:1
Born of a virgin	Isaiah 7:14	Matthew 1:18, 24-25
Declared to be the Son of God	Psalm 2:7	Matthew 3:17
Preceded by a messenger	Isaiah 40:3 Malachi 3:1, 11:10	Matthew 3:1-3
Sold for 30 pieces of silver	Zechariah 11:12	Matthew 26:15, 27:3
Heal blind/deaf/lame/dumb	Isaiah 29:18, 32:3-4	Matthew 9:32-35, 11:4-6
Wounded for our sins	Isaiah 53:5	John 6:51
His body was pierced	Psalm 22:16	Luke 23:33, John 20:25-27
No bones broken	Psalm 34:20	John 19:33-36
Resurrected from the dead	Psalm 16:10-11 Mark 16:6	Acts 2:31
Ascended to heaven	Psalm 68:18	Acts 1:9 Luke 24:51

Likewise, the Bible gives many prophetic signs that predict and foretell of Jesus' Second Coming and the End of the Age. The Bible, and only the Bible, reveals the great and final scenes of our world's history. Events that are happening today are precursors to the events of the future. As so many prophetic events have already occurred, there is every good reason to think that other prophecies made, but not yet fulfilled, will also come true.

One of the prophecies still being fulfilled states that before Jesus returns, there will be an increase in travel and knowledge. Daniel 12:4 says *"But as for you, Daniel, conceal these words and seal up the book until the end of time; many will go back and forth, and knowledge will increase".* This prophecy predicts that in the End Times, more and more discoveries and knowledge will occur, and many people will better understand the prophecies in the books of Daniel and Revelation.

Today there is more interest in understanding these prophetic books of the Bible, especially since many of the prophecies are being fulfilled in our lifetime. Air travel, space travel, DNA research, animal cloning, explosion in the communication area, etc. are all examples of the increasingly rapid advancement in travel and knowledge.

Here is a comparison list of the change in speed and ease of around the world travel over the centuries:

- In 1519, Ferdinand Magellan set sail in September and completed the first voyage around the world three years later in September, 1522.
- In 1890, Nellie Bly, an American newspaper reporter, completed a record trip around the world in 72 days 6 hours 11 minutes.
- In 1924, two U.S. Army Airplanes flew around the earth in 363 hours 7 minutes (15.1) days.
- In 1933, Wiley Post made the first solo flight around the world in 7 days 18 hours 49 minutes.
- In 1949, Lucky Lady II, a U.S. Air Force bomber, made the first nonstop flight around the world in 94 hours (3.9 days), being refueled in flight four times.
- In 1962, John Glenn, Jr., a U.S. astronaut, circled the earth in 1 & 1/2 hours.

Since the flight of John Glenn, Jr., we have built even faster, more efficient spacecraft and airplanes, including the Shuttle. It can be said that travel, both in terms of distance and in speed, as well as the ease of people to travel around the world ("back and forth") have increased as Daniel predicted!

Yet another of God's prophecies not yet finally fulfilled is that the Word will be spread to the whole world prior to His return. Matthew 24:14 states, "*This gospel of the kingdom shall be preached in the whole world as a testimony to all the nations, and then the end will come.*"

This prophecy is being fulfilled right now through television, radio, satellite, missionaries, the translation of the Bible into many languages, the internet, social media, etc. People all over the world can now hear the message of Christ through missionaries who have the ability to travel to all parts of the globe. Advances in technology make it possible to communicate with people on the other side of the world right from our own homes, churches and offices.

The following stories show how these prophecies are being fulfilled today, and how God continues to make sure His plan is carried out as He designed it to be.

Increase in Travel and Knowledge

Communion on the Moon

Landing on the moon would have been impossible and incredible for the people in the 1850s. Yet, just a little over a hundred years later, man went from riding in a stage coach to landing on the moon, 235,000 miles from earth! The amount of knowledge increase that occurred in that short amount of time is truly remarkable! This increase in knowledge continues to this day, resulting in such innovations as the iPad, smart phones, wireless communication, more sophisticated rockets, DNA research, medical advances, etc.

It was Christmas Eve 1968 when astronauts William Anders, James Lovell and the commander of the mission, Colonel Frank Borman, became the first astronauts to circle the moon. As they did so in Apollo 8, they each broadcast back to earth portions from the first book of the Bible, Genesis 1:1-10.

William Anders: "We are approaching lunar sunrise, and for all the people back on Earth, the crew of Apollo 8 has a message that we would like to send to you."

'In the beginning God created the heaven and the earth. And the earth was without form and void; and darkness was upon the face of the deep. And the Spirit of God moved upon the face of the waters. And God said, Let there be light; and there was light. And God saw the

light, that it was good; and God divided the light from the darkness (Genesis 1:1-4 KJV)."

Jim Lovell

"And God called the light Day, and the darkness he called Night. And the evening and the morning were the first day. And God said, Let there be a firmament in the midst of the waters, and let it divide the waters from the waters. And God made the firmament and divided the waters which were under the firmament from the waters which were above the firmament; and it was so. And God called the firmament Heaven. And the evening and the morning were the second day (Genesis 1:5-8 KJV)."

Frank Borman

And God said, Let the waters under the heaven be gathered together unto one place, and let the dry land appear; and it was so. And God called the dry land Earth; and the gathering together of the waters called the Seas; and God saw it was good (Genesis 1:9-10 KJV)."

Commander Borman added:

"We close with good night, good luck, a Merry Christmas, and God bless all of you—all of you on the good Earth."[1]

Atheist Madalyn Murray O'Hare was outraged by this broadcast. She filed suit against the United States government, alleging violations of the first amendment. The next year on July 20, 1969, Apollo astronauts Buzz Aldrin and Neil Armstrong landed on the moon. Before stepping onto the moon's surface, Buzz asked to broadcast the astronauts' celebration of communion. He was told by NASA (National Aeronautics and Space Administration) that was not possible because of the pending lawsuit by O'Hare.

The two astronauts shared the communion together anyway in the lunar lander and then exited to the moon's surface.

O'Hare's lawsuit was later dismissed by the Supreme Court. Subsequently, Buzz Aldrin wrote about the communion event in the October, 1970, monthly publication of *Guideposts*. The lunar landing was re-enacted in the 1998 Emmy winning HBO mini-series, *From the Earth to the Moon* starring Tom Hanks, and co-produced by Tom Hanks, Ron Howard, Brian Grazer, and Michael Bostick.

Madalyn Murray O'Hare wanted to put a stop to any religious activity or references in space. She was denied that attempt. The publicity that has been generated by music, writings and movies of this and other space achievements has far exceeded any suppression of religion that she tried to make happen.

Isaiah 55:11 states: *"So will My word be which goes forth from My mouth; it will not return to Me empty, without accomplishing what I desire, and without succeeding in the matter for which I sent it."*

God's word won that battle!

Adding to the irony is that Madalyn Murray O'Hare's own son, William Murray, became a devout Christian. He founded a Christian ministry, The Religious Freedom Coalition. More information can be found on his website: www.religiousfreedomcoalition.org/.

EARTH WITHOUT OCEANS

From the vantage point of satellites and with the aid of computer generated imaging, we can now *see* through video and animation what the earth would look like if the oceans were drained. A National Geographic television special presented a series of programs that explore what the earth under the seas would look like if drained of all water.

Technological advances such as unmanned subs and advanced mapping software have made it possible to create computer images of the ocean floors that provide the same level of detail as those secured for the surface of Mars. Ocean areas of the earth that look like swimming pools from above reveal vastly different terrain when the water is stripped away with the computer images.

For example, the waters off the Bahamas may appear to be like a huge swimming pool from the surface. This technology has revealed that below the surface are steep cliffs that rise almost two miles above the vast plain of the ocean floor. Yosemite National Park's five-thousand-foot tall Half Dome appears like a small hill in comparison.[1]

Perhaps the earth under the drained seas looks like it did when God said in Genesis 1: 1-2a: *"In the beginning God created the heavens and the earth. The earth was formless and void"* . . . Does that mean bare, dry? Void of what, water?

One day God may reveal that to us. In the meantime, man will further explore and discover, using his ever-expanding knowledge of technology and science.

Vertical Farming—New Way to Feed the World

Within the next fifty years there will be approximately three billion more people added to our planet.[1] They will need to be fed. Using current technology, it will take an area nearly the size of the United States to grow this extra food. Most of the usable land in the world is already in use. So the challenge is to find a new way to grow food.

During the last few years a process called Aeroponics[2] has grown in favor. Shortage of water supply in many areas has fueled interest in Aeroponics. This process has been explored by NASA, which is interested in it because astronauts will need to be able to grow their own food during lengthy trips to explore deep space.

Aeroponics does not use soil. Instead of using acres of land, gardens can be stacked in a multi-storied building. A wick-like cloth substitutes as soil and a mist saturates this cloth, providing all the water, nutrients and oxygen needed by the plants. In place of sunlight, the plants are grown using solar powered LED lights.

Some of the advantages of growing food using Aeroponics are listed below.[3]

1. The need for land is substantially reduced.
2. Vegetables are grown in a self contained and controlled environment so weather problems such as drought, hail, storms, erosion of the soil, lack of sunshine, etc., are eliminated.
3. Food can be grown all year. This results in shorter growing cycles. Instead of only two crops of tomatoes per year, the vertical farming process can yield six crops.

4. Spoilage is reduced and shelf life is greatly increased.
5. Evaporation is eliminated and the need for water is dramatically reduced.
6. Since food can be grown nearly anywhere (even in urban areas), the cost of transportation is reduced and the need for gasoline is also decreased.
7. Food grown without the need for soil eliminates soil borne diseases. This results in the food being cleaner and more sanitary.
8. Plants still give off some residue, but this residue can be converted into energy. The energy produced is enough to power the LED lighting. This makes the vertical farm nearly self-sustaining.
9. LEDs allow more even distribution of lighting and permit focused wavelengths of light.
10. The need for fertilizer (made from petrochemicals) is eliminated.
11. Vertical farming can be done using existing structures, thus permitting redevelopment of squalid areas.
12. People can live and work in the city.
13. This type of farming will attract a different type of farmer, and the labor force will be more educated.
14. Vertical farming eliminates the need for pesticides, herbicides and fungicides. Pests are not an issue because the food is grown inside a controlled space.
15. Food grown using vertical farming contains more nutrients and vitamins and is healthier and less expensive.
16. This controlled-environment farming is safer than traditional farming because it eliminates the sources of most farm accidents, which are caused by machinery,

tools and exposure to chemicals such as fungicides and pesticides.
17. Food grown in a controlled environment improves food safety and lessens the need for food inspection, because there is much less exposure to diseases like E. coli, salmonella, etc.
18. Vertical farming does not depend on political stability in other countries to grow and export food.
19. A vertical farm can be configured so that vegetables can even be grown underground. It is speedy to build and install.

There are only a few negatives about vertical farming. It is untested; farmers will require new skills and education to farm this way; not all plants can be grown with aeroponics, resulting in less variety of food.

Is this part of the "increase in knowledge" in the Latter Days spoken about in Daniel 12:4? No one knows for sure, but it just could be.

Gospel Translated for the World

A detailed database maintained by Ethnologue, www.ethnologue.com, estimates there are approximately 6,900 known living languages in the world.[1] Statistics available from 1997 affirmed that portions of the Bible had been translated into 2,197 different languages.[2]

As commerce and trade come to many more people around the world, dialects and languages die out and other established languages take their place. It is estimated by the United Nations that nearly 3,000 of the world's languages and dialects are dying.[3]

If these nearly 3,000 languages and dialects will be gone, and portions of the Gospel are already translated into almost 2,200 languages, then only about 1,700 languages still need translation. Many small countries, like Papua New Guinea, have hundreds of different dialects and languages and make up more than half of the languages yet to be translated. Yet, their population total is only a small percentage of the total population of the world.

The Bible continues to be the most translated book in the world. With the help of computers the Bible can now be translated even more quickly, and a greater number of people are able to have a Bible in a language they know. The completion of Bible translation and its availability to all peoples around the world is approaching realization.

Jesus said, "*This gospel of the kingdom shall be preached in the whole world as a testimony to all the nations, and then the end will come*" (Matthew 24:14).

Apps are now offered for smart phones and other devices that allow users to read the Bible with easy access. They are increasingly available in more and more languages. Many offer a daily reading plan, a verse-of-the-day display, and other special features. Many app versions make it possible to switch between Bible versions for comparison and clarification.

This increase in knowledge is another way God is fulfilling His great commission to proclaim the Gospel to the whole world.

TWEETING FOR GOD

Unlike some who use Twitter and Facebook for distasteful messages and self-serving purposes, Congressman John Shimkus from Illinois posts daily Bible verses on his official Congressional Twitter and Facebook accounts.

He was skeptical at first about using social networking in this way, but saw how some other members used it successfully and tastefully to communicate with others. The sites have provided a means for the Congressman to share his faith with others. He believes that God has a great plan and places people where they are so that His will and purpose will be accomplished.

The Congressman says, "I am a Christian by faith. I believe in God's role in our daily life".[1] He feels a great responsibility to do his best for his constituents, as well as for God. The devotionals he sends keeps him grounded in his daily life and strengthens his faith by reminding him of the principles that the Bible teaches.

Ephesians 2:8-9 is Shimkus' favorite Bible verse.[2] *"For by grace you have been saved through faith; and that not of yourselves, it is the gift of God; not as a result of works, so that no one may boast."*

FINDING OIL AND GAS IN ISRAEL

Large quantities of oil and natural gas have been discovered in Israel.[1] So why is this important? Israel is only a small country about the size of the state of New Jersey, but it is at the center of the world. The world revolves around it. Could these discoveries be another example of a continuing increase in knowledge fulfilling God's prophecy?

An understanding of the significance of these oil and gas discoveries requires a review of some biblical history. The following Bible verses describe God's promises to reveal and provide tremendous wealth for Israel in the Last Days. The passages below were probably passed on orally from generation to generation and then written down several thousand years ago.

Deuteronomy 33:24 (As said of Asher, the 8th son of Jacob)[2]

> *"More blessed than sons is Asher. May he be favored by his brothers, and may he dip his foot in oil."*

Genesis 49:25

> *"From the God of your father who helps you, and by the Almighty who blesses you with blessings of heaven above, blessings of the deep that lies beneath."*

Deuteronomy 33:13 (As said of Joseph)

> *"Blessed of the Lord be his land, with the choice things of heaven, with the dew, and from the deep lying beneath."*

Deuteronomy 33:19

"They will call peoples to the mountain. There they will offer righteous sacrifices, for they will draw out the abundance of the seas, and the hidden treasures of the sand."

Deuteronomy 32:12-13

"The Lord alone guided him, (Israel) and there was no foreign god with him. He made him ride on the high places of the earth, and he ate the produce of the field. And he made him suck honey from the rock, and oil from the flinty rock."

Isaiah 45:3

"I will give you the treasures of darkness and hidden wealth of secret places, so that you may know that it is I, the Lord, the God of Israel, who calls you by your name."

In Daniel 12:4 the angel Michael told Daniel, *"Conceal these words and seal up the book until the end of time; many will go back and forth, and knowledge will increase."* When this verse is linked with those above, I believe it shows how God is fulfilling prophecy and more and more rapidly unveiling His plan for the world as the time of His return draws nearer.

Drilling for oil in Israel was first done in the late 1940s in an area south of Tel Aviv near Ashkelon.[3] In 1952, in order to attract other exploration to provide for Israel's energy needs, Israel's parliament enacted a bill into law[4] that gave attractive incentives to companies which would come to Israel and drill. These incentives included low taxes and low royalty payments to the government. Oil was discovered in 1955, but the size of the discovery was not significant. Other small oil companies continued to drill. They discovered a few oil fields, but these, too, were not commercially viable.

Arab states like Saudi Arabia, Iraq, etc. have always boycotted the sale of oil to Israel because of their great animosity toward the Jews. With no energy source of its own, Israel was forced to import oil from Russia, Kazakhstan and Azerbaijan, and coal from South Africa.

In 1967 Egypt, Jordan, and Syria attacked Israel in the conflict called The Six Day War. Against all odds Israel won decisively, but the conflict depleted Israel's armaments. Because the United States resupplied arms to Israel, the oil-producing Arab nations retaliated against the United States by decreasing oil production. This led to increases in the price of oil and resulted in the 1973 oil shortage crisis in the United States. It also intensified Israel's interest in finding its own oil supply. The country presently imports 98% of its energy needs.[5]

In addition to drilling on land, exploration for oil expanded off the coast of Israel into the waters of the Mediterranean. In the 1980s Israel tried government-owned drilling but gave up and returned to a policy of letting private companies do the work of exploration. This attracted even more drilling.[6]

Meanwhile, drilling technology improved. Horizontal drilling versus vertical drilling was further developed and more widely used. There are advantages and disadvantages of both types, but horizontal drilling has made it possible to drill where vertical drilling would not have been feasible. Additionally, new ways to extract oil from shale were devised. Between 1998 and 2008 some other oil discoveries were made, but these were small in terms of the amount of oil that was produced.

The discovery of an onshore oil site was made in 2010 in northern Israel by the exploration company Givot Olam.[7] The company based its search for oil in Israel on Scripture. This Meged 5 field site, located near Rosh Ha'ayin, has a potential of huge quantities of oil. Drilling continues to develop a commercially viable way to extract it.

Further advances were made when the process by which natural gas could be liquefied was invented.[8] Liquefaction of natural gas made it easier to transport and less susceptible to sabotage attempts. In early 2009 a monster find of natural gas was discovered fifty-five miles west of the port of Haifa in the Mediterranean. It was called the Tamar field.[9] This was followed a few months later by a find twice as large in the Mediterranean between Israel and Cyprus called Leviathan.[10]

To put these discoveries into perspective, they are nearly twice the size of what the British have found in the North Sea.[11] The Texas-based company, Noble Energy, has since discovered a gargantuan deposit of natural gas in the Leviathan Field, buried a mile beneath the ocean floor. This Israeli find, estimated at some 16 trillion cubic feet, is large enough that Prime Minister Benjamin Netanyahu commented in a CNN interview with Piers Morgan in March, 2011, that Israel might forego building nuclear reactors and rely on generations of natural energy instead.[12]

Besides these two major offshore discoveries, plans are being made to exploit Israel's massive shale oil deposits in the Shfela Basin,[13] located about thirty miles southwest of Jerusalem. Just the gas finds here could make Israel self-sufficient in natural gas for decades. If successful, Israel would be catapulted into the energy superpower league. Israel could become a major exporter of energy!

If so, Saudi Arabia and other oil exporters have plenty to worry about. Until now, extortion and the threat of a boycott in retaliation for loyalty to Israel have allowed them to dictate foreign policy to other countries including the United States. Recent changes and government instability in many of the Arab countries in the Middle East have caused the world's oil supply to be unstable.

Israel and Lebanon have not been able to agree on geographical borders and a territorial squabble has developed for the finds discovered in the Mediterranean. Backed by Syria, Iran and other Arab countries, including the terrorist organization of Hezbollah, Lebanon has laid claim to the discoveries.

Additionally, Israel's Parliament has retroactively rewritten the 1952 law resulting in increased taxes and royalties.[14] Drilling and exploration companies are not pleased with this.

God has promised the land of Israel great riches from the "deep". These discoveries of oil and natural gas may fulfill these promises to Israel made in the Old Testament. The significance of these discoveries and developments cannot be denied or diminished in their importance, and I believe they are a direct result of the increase in knowledge as predicted in Daniel 12:4.

Papyrus to Pixels

The finding of the Dead Sea Scrolls has been called the greatest archaeological find of the 20th century.[1] The Scrolls were discovered by Bedouin teenagers in late 1946 or early 1947 in an area located on the northwest shore of the Dead Sea (near the present-day West Bank).

One of the young shepherds tossed a rock into a cave opening on the side of a cliff and was surprised to hear a shattering sound when the rock landed. Curious to know what was in the cave, the teenagers climbed into the opening and found several large clay jars that held scrolls made of leather and papyrus.

Eventually eleven caves were found, containing thousands of additional pieces of scrolls.[2] Scholars have estimated many of the texts to be around two thousand years old. To date 825-870 separate scrolls have been identified by scholars from those that were uncovered. Among them are nineteen copies of the Book of Isaiah, thirty copies of Psalms, and twenty-five copies of Deuteronomy.[3] The Isaiah Scroll, which was found relatively intact, is a thousand years older than any previously known copy of Isaiah.[4] Other manuscripts were found to be relatively intact in Caves 1 and 11. In 1952 Cave 4 was discovered, and it produced the largest find—five hundred manuscripts that contained fifteen thousand fragments.[5]

The area where the Scrolls were hidden is very arid with low humidity, making the climate very conducive to their preservation. Even so, many of the Scrolls survived only as tiny fragments. Many are so brittle and fragile, that great care must be taken in handling them. Direct light is not allowed to shine on them.[6]

The Copper Scroll, discovered in Cave 3, contains records of sixty-four underground hiding places located throughout Judea (none of which have been found!). Unlike all of the other scrolls made of leather or parchment, it is made entirely of copper and had to be cut in strips to be opened. It could be the greatest treasure map in history. The monetary value of the Copper Scroll is close to $3 billion—its historical value is priceless.[7]

The hiding places contained treasures from the Temple of Jerusalem, like gold, silver, aromatics and other manuscripts, hidden away for safekeeping. One of the editors of the Dead Sea Scrolls, Stephen Pfann, has said: "This is a tremendous witness to history. To actually have a list of treasures from the temple itself from the first century is just amazing. We have nothing better than the Copper Scroll now for telling us what was really there."[8]

The majority of the Dead Sea Scrolls are written in Hebrew.[9] Several are written in Aramaic, and a few texts are written in Greek. Aramaic was the common language of the Jews during the last two centuries B.C. and the first two centuries A.D. Jesus most likely spoke Aramaic. The Scrolls were written between 150 B.C. and 70 A.D., and they contain both biblical and non-biblical content. Except for the book of Esther, fragments of every book of the Old Testament have been found.[10]

Who wrote them is still debated among scholars. However, the prevailing theory is that they were written by a communal group of devout and ascetic Jews called the Essenes.[11] There is evidence the sect lived in Qumran (the area where the scrolls were found) until the Romans destroyed their settlement around 70 A.D. Descriptions in the Scroll mention a sect living then. A historical description of the Essenes by the Roman historian, Flavius Josephus, further verifies their existence.

A study of the Scrolls has revealed that the Bible has not changed in content down through the ages as many skeptics had surmised.[12] *"The words of the Lord are pure words; as silver tried in a furnace on the earth, refined seven times. You, O Lord, will keep them; You will preserve him from this generation forever"* (Psalm 12:6-7).

Many of the Scrolls are housed in the world-class Israel Museum, which opened in May, 1965. Its most popular section is the dimly-lighted Shrine of the Book. American architects Kiesler and Bartos designed it with a distinctive onion-shaped top, meant to resemble the covers of the jars in which the Dead Sea Scrolls were discovered.[13] The dome sits atop a structure which is two-thirds below the ground. This structure is reflected in the pool of water that surrounds it. The Shrine of the Book houses the "best preserved and most complete Dead Sea Scrolls ever discovered", states Israel Museum director James Snyder.[14] Its featured showcase is located beneath the dome and is shaped like a wooden Torah rod. It contains a facsimile of the Great Isaiah Scroll, thought to be written in 100 B.C. Sixty-six chapters are displayed on a twenty-three foot long, sewn-together piece of parchment.[15] Also on display are the Psalms Scroll and the Temple Scroll. The artifacts are displayed on a rotational basis to minimize damage from exposure.

Since their discovery the Dead Sea Scrolls have created a heated controversy among antiquities scholars about access to the scrolls and the push to speed up their publication. The staff of the Department of Artefacts' Treatment and Conservation at the Israeli Antiquities Authority want to be responsive to the intense interest, but must limit the time a scroll is exposed to light, humidity and heat to prevent further deterioration. Even without exposure there is continued deterioration because of the ink used on some of the Scrolls, as well as harm done by some scholars in the 1950s who attempted to piece fragments together with the use of Scotch tape.[16]

Infrared cameras were used in the 1950s to photograph the entire collection. These photographs are stored in a climate-controlled room. They verify that some things have already been lost from the Scrolls.

On September 27, 2011, an announcement was made about a $3.5 million joint project between the Israel Museum and Google to put five of the eight Scrolls housed in the museum on-line! These five Scrolls, containing some of the oldest-known surviving biblical texts, have been digitized with the latest technology. This makes them available on-line for anyone to see. The ancient texts that have been digitized are: The Great Isaiah Scroll; the Community Rule Scroll, the Commentary on Habbakuk, the Temple Scroll, and the War Scroll.[17]

When on-line and viewing the Scrolls, one can simply scroll over the phrases of one of the Scrolls and the words are instantly translated into English!! The official Google blog stated, "It's taken 24 centuries, the work of archaeologists, scholars and historians, and the Internet to make the Dead Sea Scrolls accessible to anyone in the world."[18] Besides providing an English translation tool, Google also has an option for users to submit translations of verses in their own languages. A Chinese translation is also in the works. Additionally, there are plans to scan in and make available for viewing the old infrared pictures of the 1950s.

God has indeed preserved the integrity of His Word through generation after generation. Previously these important archaeological documents were only available to a privileged few.

Now He is spreading the Word to all by making viewing of the Scrolls more easily accessible on any computer, anywhere in the world. They are viewable on the web site http://dss.collections.imj.org.il/. The twelve hundred megapixels resolution offers amazing clarity that has made the images much sharper than any that could be made by today's best professional cameras.[19] It is even possible to see how thin and fragile the parchment and animal skin of the original scrolls are.

There are plans to make more of the Dead Sea Scrolls available through this technique. This is another special and fantastic way that God is spreading His unchanging, mighty Word and working in today's world.

"The grass withers, the flower fades, but the word of our God stands forever." Isaiah 40:8

Reaching Nations With The Gospel

In Matthew 24:3 Jesus was asked by His disciples, *"Tell us, when will these things happen, and what **will be** the sign of Your coming, and of the end of the age?"*

Jesus told His disciples that no one knows the day or the hour of His return; that even He (Jesus) did not know; that only God the Father knows. Jesus then gave them some general information that would foretell when He would come again, and then said in Matthew 24:14:

> *"This gospel of the kingdom shall be preached in the whole world as a testimony to all the nations, and then the end will come."*

There is not just one way that God's Word is spread—there are a myriad of ways through which the Gospel is preached, taught, read and experienced. The following stories tell about some of these ways. These stories are varied in their content, location and circumstance. They show how God is working to make His Word known to all and to bring His plan to fruition.

The Gospel Made Known by Bibles

The Gideons International is a phenomenal organization. It was founded in 1899 and is an extension and non-competing missionary arm of the church. It is the oldest and possibly the only interdenominational Christian business and professional men's association in the United States. One of its requirements for membership is that an applicant be a member in good standing of a Protestant church and have the recommendation of his pastor.

The Gideon's story began in the fall of 1898, when two Wisconsin salesmen traveled separately to Boscobel, Wisconsin. They did not know one another, but they both decided to stay for the night at the same hotel in the town. There was only one room in the inn, so they (John Nicholson from Janesville and Samuel Hill from Beloit) shared a hotel room. When the two men discovered they were both Christians, they had their evening devotions together. While on their knees before God thoughts were given to them which later resulted in formation of an association.

Only three men were at the first official meeting on July 1, 1899, at the YMCA in Janesville, Wisconsin. They were Samuel E. Hill, who became president; Will J. Knights, named Vice President; and John H. Nicholson, secretary and treasurer. The Gideon organization was born.

The name was taken from the story about Gideon in the sixth and seventh chapters of the book of Judges in the Old Testament. Gideon was a man who was willing to do exactly what God wanted him to do, regardless of what he, himself, wanted or planned to do. Humility, faith and obedience were the great elements of his character.

This is the standard The Gideons International tries to establish in all its members. Each man is to be ready to do God's Will at any time, at any place, and in any way that the Holy Spirit leads.

Nearly all of the Gideons in the early years of the association were traveling salesmen. Since the members traveled a great deal, it was natural that they would search for a way they could effectively witness in the hotels where they spent so much time. One trustee boldly suggested that the Gideons supply a Bible for each hotel room in all of the United States. This plan, called "The Bible Project", was set in motion in 1908.

At a regional convention held a few months later in Cedar Rapids, Iowa, there was a plea made for the monetary need to support this Bible distribution program. One of the pastors attending the convention, Dr. E. R. Burkhalter of First Presbyterian Church of Cedar Rapids, suggested that the member churches in the organization provide and place Gideon Bibles in all local hotels. The proposal was voted on and passed, and a committee was formed to allocate the cost of Bibles.

Today the Gideons rely on donations from churches and individuals to support the distribution of Bibles and New Testaments. Dues collected from members cover the administration costs of the organization. One hundred percent of the donations received are used to purchase and distribute Bibles.

The complete Bible is distributed in hotels; the Testaments are pocket-sized and are made up of the New Testament, Proverbs and Psalms. They include a section of "Helps" (where to find help when anxious, angry, etc) with page numbers in the front of the book. The "Plan of Salvation" is located on the last two pages.

Just over one hundred years ago, the first Gideon Bibles were placed in the rooms at the Superior Hotel in Superior, Montana. Today, Gideons not only place Bibles in hotels, but also in hospitals and prisons and large-print editions in nursing homes. Additionally, they distribute Testaments to school children around-the-world. This is all done by individual Gideons. At hotels they go room to room, replacing Bibles that are worn with new ones. When possible the old Bibles are restored with a soft cover and re-distributed in prisons.

During World War II the Gideons were asked by the military to provide Testaments for military men and women. Bibles that have desert camouflaged covers are available today and are distributed by Gideons at local military induction services. Besides those for the military, Gideons provide Testaments in various colors as noted below:

Orange:	For sidewalk (off-campus) distribution to middle/high school students
Green:	For college/university students
Red:	For in-school distribution to Middle/High School students
Dark blue:	For law enforcement personnel, firefighters, and EMTs
White:	For medical professionals in hospitals and doctors' offices
Brown:	Personal worker's testaments (for Gideon witness to individuals)
Periwinkle:	Personal worker's testaments (for Gideon witness to individuals)

The Gideons principally use the *King James Version* for their Bibles, because there is no copyright cost involved. The ministry provides Bibles in one hundred ninety countries and in ninety languages. To date, with God's grace and blessing, they have provided upwards of 1.6 billion Bibles and Testaments and put God's Word within the reach of nearly one sixth of the world's population. There are 290,000 Gideons and Auxiliary (wives of Gideons) members. All are volunteer and unpaid. There are nearly ten thousand camps (local organizations) around the world. Gideons are like missionaries as they spread God's word to parts of the world where the Bible would not otherwise be known or available.[1]

On average, more than two copies of God's Word are distributed by the Gideons per second. Millions of people around the world struggle to survive and can't afford to buy much of anything, let alone a book. For example, in Zimbabwe inflation has increased costs to the extreme, and it would be years before many there would be able to buy any book, let alone a Bible. Because the Gideon New Testaments and Bibles are free to the recipient, those who might never be able to read the Word are provided with a means to do so—and in their own language.

The mission of the Gideons is a great example of how God works in today's world. Following are testimonies of people brought to Christ through the receiving of Bibles distributed by the Gideons. These Gideon stories are designated by the letter "G" at the end of the title of each story. In a few instances the testimonies may have been edited to clarify it for the reader, but in no way has the intent and meaning of the testimony been changed. More information is available on the Gideon website: www.gideons.org.

BIBLES FALL FROM THE SKY!ᴳ

The following story was told by Alexi T., pastor of the evangelical Christian Baptist Church in Noyabrisk, Siberia.

"Several years ago, a hungry Nemets fisherman left the town of Ceaca on the Yamal Peninsula in Siberia. The Nemets are hunters and fishermen who live on the Siberian tundra. This fisherman went looking for food, and he prayed to any god who might hear him, asking for a sign.

Not long after he finished his prayer, a Bible fell from the sky and landed near him. He went back into town with the Bible saying, "I have received a sign." Today, he is part of a church where there are thirty Nemets Christians.

What the villager did not know is that a helicopter had flown from Slaekhard the day he got his sign. In that helicopter were two government officials bringing relief aid to needy areas. As they flew, they sorted through their cargo. One said to the other, "The cans of food are good, but what do we need with these books?" So they began throwing Gideon Bibles out of the window."[1]

Note: It may not have been a miracle of God that the Bible fell beside that fisherman just at that instant. But, it was an act of obedience that put the Bible on the helicopter in the first place. Christians paid money to have those Bibles printed; they paid to have them delivered to Siberia. Others were praying that the Gospel would find good soil among the Nemets people. God used their faithfulness, their commitment to His mission, and their love for the Nemets people to get His Word to them.

MEETING GOD UNDER THE OCEAN

"Stan F. was born and raised on an island off the coast of Maine. The island was predominantly inhabited by first and second generation Irish immigrants.

Following graduation from high school, he went to a Navy boot camp in Illinois. While there he received a Gideon Testament from the local Gideons. It got shoved into his sea bag, and there it stayed for several years.

Years into his Navy career Stan's life was in shambles. He had begun to drink heavily, and his marriage was in trouble. He began searching for answers, as he realized something was missing in his life—it was void of meaning and purpose.

One day, in a submarine off the Atlantic coast, Stan remembered the New Testament he received in boot camp and removed it from his sea bag. He says, "I began to read and found in that New Testament things I never knew before. I found that while I was still a sinner, God loved me and sent His Son Jesus Christ to die for me. And there, four hundred feet under the ocean, I surrendered my life to the Lord Jesus Christ."[1]

"If I ascend to heaven, You are there; If I make my bed in Sheol, behold, You are there. If I take the wings of the dawn, if I dwell in the remotest part of the sea, even there, Your hand will lead me, and Your right hand will lay hold of me" (Psalm 139:8-10).

A Grandmother's Last Words—"Don't Wait"[G]

"Harold's life was out of control. Seeking some stability in his life, he joined the Navy. While in boot camp he heard two other servicemen talking about how they were looking forward to going home for the holidays and enjoying Christmas church services. Inspired, Harold decided that when he got home to Iowa for the holidays, he would also go to church with his family.

"But when Christmas Eve came, he went drinking with some buddies instead of attending church. That night his grandmother suffered a stroke. Harold went to visit her on Christmas day with a guilty conscience. As he was leaving to return to his base, she spoke her last words to him, 'Don't wait until you're old to give your life to Christ. Do it while you are still young.'

"A short time later he happened to encounter a Gideon who was distributing service Testaments near the naval base. Pricked in the heart by his grandmother's stern warning, Harold grabbed the Testament he had been given and returned to his bunk at the base. As he read the New Testament and book of Psalms, God's Word began to speak to him. Soon he asked Christ to be his Savior. Harold continued to grow in his relationship with the Lord. He eventually was called into the ministry and even became an ordained elder in his church."[1]

FROM DEEP DESPAIR TO THE MOUNTAINTOP^G

"I lived on a farm in the southeastern part of Iowa, near the mighty Mississippi River. My family was a hard-working family, but they did not take time out every Sunday to attend Sunday School. Our church was small—only about twenty people attended. We had worship services just once a month. I could handle that. During the week, God was never mentioned in our home. I never heard a prayer. It was like God was put on a shelf until the following Sunday.

"When I married, our life was much the same. We attended church once in a while. Our lives were devoted to work. We had a nice living, did lots of traveling, had the material things we wanted, but I always felt there was something more to life. On January 5, 1982, our lives changed. Our youngest son, Shawn, age sixteen, took his own life. I cannot describe the pain and loss I felt or what it did to our family. All those things that seemed so important before now meant nothing. We left our business, home, and friends, and we ran.

"In the next years, we lived in many states and tried many different jobs—always quitting because we couldn't handle them. My husband and I could not comfort each other, because we were both filled with so much pain. Once we had been a very close couple; now we became distant. Most of our conversation was talking about taking our own lives.

"My husband started building motels for a motel chain. I did the setting up of the rooms and the hiring and training of personnel. I worked long, hard hours. That way I was too tired to think. Because of back injuries, I soon could no longer walk without pain. I couldn't work, so I spent many hours in the motel room where we lived.

"I had noticed that in the room there was a Bible placed by the Gideons. I had no idea who they were. I started looking at the Bible, but didn't know where to start reading. I looked at the first page and read, "Help in Time of Need." I needed help. I couldn't get over the pain of losing my son; my marriage was falling apart; I couldn't work because of my back; my husband's health was failing also; and the doctors said we both needed surgery. We could not escape from our pain.

"As I began to read the verses, I realized Jesus could be my Comforter, Healer and Counselor. During the following days, I poured out my heart to Him. All the feelings I had been unable to share with others came out.

"One night I had a beautiful dream in which I saw my son. He had a big smile on his face, and I heard him say that he was happy. When I awoke, I felt a heavy weight had been lifted from my shoulders and my horrible chest pain was gone.

"When my husband left the motel room, I took out the Bible from its hiding place and read again the way to salvation. When I came to Acts 16:31, I was ready to believe in the Lord Jesus Christ and be saved. I knew then that it was Jesus who had taken away my pain. I got down on my knees and asked Jesus to forgive me of my sins. I asked Him to show me the way He wanted me to live because I didn't know how.

"One day my husband said to me, 'Jean, you've changed.' Until that time I had hidden the Bible under a chair when my husband entered the room. I guess I was scared of his reaction. But this time I shared what had happened to me, and he listened. For the first time in our married life, we prayed together and began studying the Bible. It was a glorious day when I saw my husband stand up and go down the aisle to ask Jesus Christ to come into his life.

"Jesus lives in my heart each and every day. I live to serve Him. When I go through those deep, dark valleys, I don't have to run. I have discovered what Jesus can do for me. I know He'll be by my side, lifting me up to the mountaintop."[1]

DEVIL WORSHIPER BECOMES A CHRISTIAN^G

David Berkowitz, known as "Son of Sam", tells his story.

"I am sitting in a prison cell. Maximum security prisons have been my home now for almost twenty years. You see, at one time I was a devil worshiper. I was living such an evil and wicked life, that I was actually seeking out demonic entities to communicate with them and in turn receive their powers.

I became in the most literal sense a servant and soldier for Satan. I took innocent lives, and I am so deeply sorry for that. I would do anything to go back in time to change things, but it is too late. I was such a fool. Not only did I destroy the lives of others, but I also threw away my life. Now I am doing more than three hundred years behind bars, serving six consecutive life sentences with no hope of ever being paroled.

"I would be the first one to tell you I deserve this sentence. Even more so, I deserve death! There were many times when I could have died. My life could have ended in 1977 when a platoon of police officers surrounded me with guns drawn. One sudden move, and I would have been blasted into eternity.

"I could have died in 1979 when, while I was confined to the infamous Attica prison, another inmate slit my throat with a razor blade. There were many other times when I dodged death.

"Through it all, I tried as best I could to get adjusted to prison life. It has been hard. Most of the time, I battled feelings of depression and loneliness. I had already been confined for ten years; I began to think I no longer had a reason to live.

"One cold winter's night I was walking in the prison yard. Another inmate walked up to me, introduced himself, and boldly told me that Jesus Christ loved me and had a plan for my life. I noticed he had a big smile on this face and a little Bible in his hands.

"After he said those words, I laughed and told him there was no way God could love me. I was too evil, and he was wasting his time. Yet this guy had such a friendly and compassionate attitude, that even though I had instantly rejected what he said, I also felt drawn to him. I guess I was hurting deep inside.

"The inmate's name was Rick, and we quickly became friends. As we walked the yard, he told me he was a Christian. I told him I was a Jew. He said it didn't matter—we have all sinned and fallen short of God's glory. Rick explained to me that we all need a Savior, there is no such thing as a righteous person, and that God loves everyone.

"Oftentimes, Rick would read portions of his New Testament to me as we walked. Within a few weeks, he gave me a small Gideon New Testament with Psalms and Proverbs. He told me to read the Psalms, that God had a *special message* just for me.

"I took that little Bible and began to read it. Late at night, when it got quiet, I would pick out a Psalm at random. I was amazed! I had never before read the Bible. The words were so beautiful. I read about King David's struggles and sufferings as he poured out his heart to God. The Psalms were full of his pain as well as his praise. As I read, it seemed as if God was indeed talking to me.

"One night it happened. It was close to midnight, and I was alone in my cell. I was looking at Psalm 34, and when I came to verse six it said, *"This poor man cried, and the Lord heard him and saved him out of all his troubles."* It was at that moment that my heart began to burst. The words pierced my soul. Everything seemed to hit me at once; all the guilt I had inside me, the anger, shame, my feelings of being a failure, my loneliness and deep hurts—everything.

"I shut off the light in my cell. Then in the darkness I felt a compelling desire to get down on my knees by my bunk and pour out my heart to God. I was filled with remorse over all the evil I had done. I began to pray, to talk with God as if He were right there in the cell with me. I asked Him to forgive me for everything I had done. I told Him how sorry I was and threw myself at the mercy of Jesus Christ.

"When I finished, I got up off my knees and felt as if a tremendous load was lifted off me. That was the moment I was born again. Although it would still take awhile to understand all that had taken place, it was the turning point in my life. I felt God's peace. For the first time in my thirty-three years on this earth, I began to experience the breaking of Satan's chains of oppression and torment.

"Now ten years have gone by. Through God's grace I am still walking with Jesus every day. I serve God at the prison I am in. I love Jesus Christ; He is not only my Savior. He is also my Lord. He has given me many wonderful Christian friends who have encouraged me and comforted me during times of trial and temptation.

"In 1987 God sent a born-again prisoner with a big smile and a little Bible into my broken-down life. Now the old things have passed away, and all things have become new. The evil "Son of Sam" has even been given a new name—"Son of Hope".

What more can I say but, "Thank you, Jesus!" [1]

Editor's Note: Berkowitz has had five parole hearings, the most recent in March, 2010. He has been denied parole all five times, all upon his request to have the parole hearings cancelled. He has said, "In all honesty, I believe that I deserve to be in prison for the rest of my life. I have, with God's help, long ago come to terms with my situation and I have accepted my punishment." Berkowitz continues to be involved in prison ministry and regularly counsels prison inmates. He receives no money from the sale of his memoir, *Son of Hope,* published in 2006. A portion of any proceeds goes to the New York State Crime Victims Board for distribution to the victims of his crimes. He is currently residing at Sullivan Correctional Facility in Fallsburg, New York, where he is a prison chaplain.

Dad Was Saved Just in Time[G]

"My dad died in a hospital for alcoholics in Chicago. We had no hope that he had made it to heaven.

"But after he died, a nurse who was making his bed found a New Testament under his mattress. That New Testament was provided by the Gideons.

"In the back of the New Testament is a page to fill out when you receive Christ as your Savior. Dad had filled it out and dated it the day before he died."[1]

HOSPITAL BIBLE COMFORTS AND SAVES татн[G]

"For three months I stayed with and waited on my husband who was dying of cancer at the Medical College of Virginia Hospital. I found a Gideon-placed Holy Bible on the dresser in the hospital and began to read it as my husband slept.

"There is absolutely nothing like the Word of the Lord! It spoke to my heart in this time of great need. I found comfort, faith and salvation.

"By the time I read through the Gospel of John, I had accepted Christ as my personal Savior. Then my husband also accepted the Lord as his Savior through the reading of the 23rd Psalm, which I read to him two weeks before he died.

"On the day he went to be with the Lord, God comforted me with Psalm 34, especially verse 4 where it states: *'I sought the Lord, and He answered me, and delivered me from all my fears.'*

"I am indeed grateful for the Bibles which are placed by Gideons everywhere—in hospitals, in hotels, in doctor's offices, in prisons . . . for the Word of God does not return void, Isaiah 55:11. Praise His wonderful name!"[1]

LEGACY OF A GRANDMOTHER'S BIBLE[G]

"My family and I eat out quite often and we always look forward to having Ava as our waitress in our favorite restaurant. She is always kind and shows us special attention. Over the course of a year, we had gotten to know her well.

"Ava knew that I was a chaplain at the county jail, and one day I received a telephone call from her. She said that her grandmother had passed away and wanted to know if I would conduct the funeral service. Ava's family was Catholic, but her grandmother had requested a Protestant service.

"I was happy to do the service, but asked if I could talk with the family beforehand. They invited me to their home, and I met with Ava and other family members. I asked Ava if her grandmother had owned a Bible, and if they still had it. She went to get it and, upon her return, handed me a well-worn Gideon Testament. It was tattered and falling apart; a rubber band held it together. It was obvious that the Testament had had a lot of use.

"I learned that Sarah, Ava's grandmother, had been a nurse in a convalescent home. One day, many years ago, an Auxiliary member (wife of a Gideon) had given her a Testament. The Testament in my hand was no longer white, but it was still beautiful.

In the back, I read that Sarah had made a confession of faith in Jesus Christ and saw where she had signed her name. She had received the Lord on April 8, 1961.

"I looked at that tattered Testament and my heart was touched. I asked the family if I could use it in the funeral service. They happily agreed.

"The Lord led me to speak on the subject of our inheritance in the Lord. I used the illustration of the Bible I had inherited from my mother. It had been carried by my grandfather a hundred years ago when he preached in a little church in Oklahoma.

"Then I showed the Gideon Testament and told Sarah's family that it was her inheritance to them. As the family listened, I told them that their grandmother would want them to know God just as she did, and I showed them where she had signed the back of the Testament.

"I asked if any of them would like to pray and accept Jesus as their Savior. Together the entire family knelt with me in the chapel and repeated a prayer of repentance as I led them. Throughout the room, people were crying and confessing their sins to Christ. Before it was over, everyone had confessed that Jesus Christ was Lord and Savior. It was a beautiful experience.

"I just wanted to let you know how the Lord used that little Testament. First He used it to save Sarah. Then after her death, He used it to reach all of her family."[1]

GOD CHANGES TAXI DRIVER'S PLANS[G]

"Herbie grew up on the streets of Manila, Philippines. At eight, he was selling cigarettes. At twelve he was addicted to drugs. At twenty-one, he was a gang leader, but his gang was busted by the police. So he decided to become a taxi driver and learn English so he could take advantage of foreigners riding in his taxi.

One day he borrowed a book from a friend. It was a Gideon New Testament. With a dictionary in hand, he studied English using the New Testament. In his desire to learn good English so he could victimize foreigners, he found Christ instead!

Herbie later held a leadership position in a prominent Scripture distribution ministry."[1]

ONE BIBLE SAVES FORTY[G]

"There was a drug lab hidden in the jungle in Colombia. In it were many chemicals, guns, and dangerous men. But this lab was different, because it also contained a Gideon New Testament.

The Testament was so popular with the forty people who were in the lab that they would argue about who would get to read it. To prevent fights, they had to draw lots so each would have time to read it.

This drug lab no longer exists, but you can find the individuals who used to work there. All forty of the people were saved from the single copy of Scripture, and twelve of them are now pastors."[1]

A Pistol or a Gideon Bible?[G]

Somewhere on the border of Oregon and California, Jack ended up in a motel room and decided there was nothing left in this life worth living for.

"I knew there had to be a God, but I didn't think that He loved me, because no one ever told me He did.

"In that motel room, I had a pistol and nothing left in life. I was bitter against law enforcement. I had to blame somebody, and decided I would shoot a policeman.

"There was a Gideon Bible on the nightstand beside the bed. I looked at that Bible and hated it. I snatched it up and threw it across the room as hard as I could. It hit the wall and fell to the floor. Then I picked it up and began to read.

"For the first time in my life, I cried out to the Lord, 'God, if you're real, don't play games with me, just help me.' I fell to my knees and started to weep. While I was on that floor weeping, a peace came into my life that I still have to this day.

"I want to give glory to the Lord Jesus Christ for what He has done in my life. And I thank and encourage you Gideons."[1]

HE STOLE A BIBLE INSTEAD OF MONEY^G

"A young man from Brazil was skilled at stealing wallets. One day, he took something that looked like a wallet full of money only to discover, when he returned to his hiding place, that it was a copy of the New Testament.

"Angry, he threw it on the ground. Yet that night, unable to sleep, he remembered the little book. He started to read the New Testament, soon abandoned his addictions, and surrendered his heart to Christ. Years later, he dedicated his life to distributing the Word."[1]

THE BOOK IS TO READ, NOT TO SMOKE^G

"A young man was in a Laotian refugee village in Thailand in 1987 and received a New Testament from a Thai Gideon. He would tear pages out of the book to roll cigarettes to smoke. After removing all the pages from one Testament, he asked for another so he could continue to smoke.

"Someone told him that the book was for him to read, not to smoke. He agreed not to use it for smoking anymore, and said that he would read it instead. Two months later, he accepted Jesus as his personal Savior.

"He returned to Laos. In November, 2008, he was very grateful to become a Gideon, so that he now has the privilege of telling others through the distribution of Scriptures about that same Jesus he found in the New Testament he was given in the refugee camp."[1]

Bank's Error Buys Bibles^G

A few years ago the local Gideon camp in Plano, Texas, ran short of money with which to buy Bibles for Testament distributions they planned to make at local schools, hotels, and hospitals. The camp members prayed about their dilemma, asking the Lord to provide a solution to the situation.

Bill Feath, a friend of mine, is a dedicated Gideon member of the Plano camp. One day he was amazed when his financial institution notified him that they had made an error of more than $1,000 in his account, in his favor! With today's computer speed and accuracy, it is very rare for a bank to make such mistakes. Bill wasn't expecting the money and felt it was God's answer to the prayers of the Gideon camp. He donated the funds to the camp towards the purchase of the needed Bibles.

Around the same time, I mentioned the shortage of funds dilemma to my Bible study class during our prayer time. At the close of the study that day a large check was handed to me by one of the members of the class. There was no longer a shortage of funds and the Testaments were able to be purchased and distributed to the local schools, hospitals and hotels.

"So I say to you, ask, and it will be given to you; seek, and you will find; knock, and it will be opened to you" (Luke 11:9).

I Thought I Was a Christian[G]

"I had always thought I was a Christian. My parents believed in God and we kept the Sabbath Day holy. We said the blessing before meals and knelt by our beds at night and recited our prayers. But I never saw a Bible in our home.

"In 1959 my husband passed away and left me with two young children. People expected me to crack up or give up, but I didn't. I had an inner strength that kept me going.

"My children and I moved to New Mexico for health purposes and were very active in our church. But when my children were in junior high, they started to doubt the religion they had been taught since childhood. Pretty soon they stopped attending church, but I couldn't break away from the rituals I had practiced all my life.

"After my yearly physical in 1977, it was discovered I had cancer. On the same day I had the biopsy, I also had a mastectomy of the right breast. By that afternoon I was sitting up and talking to visitors.

"The next day I wanted something different to read and happened to look in my nightstand. There I found a Gideon Bible. I started to read it and couldn't put it down. A feeling of joy, love, and peace came over me. I stayed in the hospital five days and all the time I was reading the Gideon Bible.

"I continued to read the Bible as I went through a month of radiation treatments and selling my house. Then my doctor said I had to take a year of chemotherapy. After nine months, I felt well enough to quit the chemotherapy. I found a new job and met a fellow worker who was a Christian. Through her I met Pastor John Powell and prayed to become a born-again Christian. I was baptized in 1984.

"I have grown so much in His Word since that day in 1977 when I discovered the Gideon Bible in my nightstand. That was the beginning of my true Christian life."[1]

Muslim Hotels Finally Welcome Bibles[G]

This story was told by a Far East Field Representative of Gideons International.

"Two Muslim owned and managed hotels had been closed to Scripture placement. The Gideons had been praying that these doors would be opened. I asked the Gideons to go with me to "knock" on these closed doors.

"A young lady manager (the daughter of the owner) of the first hotel was very accommodating. She said, 'I wanted to call a Christian church to obtain information about where I could find these books. I appreciate your coming by this morning.'

"We looked for the general manager of the second hotel, but he was not immediately available. While waiting for him, the couple who owned the hotel passed by. They were devoted Muslims. We talked to them about the Gideons and the purpose of our visit. When the Muslim manager came to meet us, we also told him the reason for our coming to the hotel.

"Before the owners left, the wife left instructions with the manager to accept Gideon Scriptures. We then placed Scriptures in the rooms as the manager accompanied us as our guide. We praise the Lord for these open doors and for the Indonesian Gideons who were willing to put feet to their prayers and go."[1]

NO ONE IS EVER TOO BAD FOR GOD'S LOVE[G]

This is a story as told by ex-con Ron Cummings.

"My Dad once told me, 'Ronnie, I think some people are just born bad.' I'm pretty positive he was talking about me. From a very young age I just seemed to gravitate toward the darker things in life, and I couldn't stay out of trouble. In my teenage years I began to run with the wrong crowd and do terrible things. When you do those types of things it's not long before you get arrested, and that's what happened to me. Everything culminated in the 1970s in the state district court in Dallas, Texas. I stood before a judge who had my file, which was very thick, and he said, 'Boy, you're never going to learn.' He sent me to the Texas prison system with sentences totaling over one hundred years.

"From the moment the judge told me that I had to serve over a hundred years in prison, my plan was to escape. You can imagine how surprised I was when the prison bus pulled up to the facility in Huntsville, Texas, and I saw the big walls, the big guard towers, and the big guns. I realized this was not going to be an easy place to get out of.

"When I found I couldn't escape physically, I chose to escape mentally—through drugs. But the problem was that drugs weren't always available, and then reality would always come rushing back in, along with the pain, the heartache and the anger.

"In 1988, I did escape. I broke out one night, and I took three pistols from the sheriff's office on the way out. My great plan was that when they caught me—and I knew they would—we would just hold court right in the middle of the street, because I had done all the time I was going to do. But God had other plans. I was surrounded and placed in leg irons and waist chains and taken back before that same judge, who was not happy. He took one look at me and said, 'Boy, you're never going to see daylight again.' He sentenced me to an additional twenty-five years.

"Late at night I began to suffer some of the most horrible nightmares you could imagine. In the one I dreamed repeatedly I was buried alive in a casket. I couldn't see and I couldn't breathe. I would kick at the bottom, but I couldn't kick it out. I would claw at the lining of this casket and panic would set in. I began to realize that I had to have some help—at least something to help me sleep.

"The doctor sent me to a psychiatrist, who determined that I was depressed. He prescribed antidepressants and sent me back to my cell block. It wasn't long before I was on anti-psychotics, and I began hearing voices that would tell me that people were out to kill me and I should kill them first. I became very aggressive.

"They took me back down to the psychiatrist and this time I was put into a straight jacket and sent to Ellis 3 Psychiatric Unit where I was stripped down and shoved into a padded cell. Each time they came to get me I would have to turn around and back up to the hole in the door so they could handcuff me. Only then would they open the main door to tranquilize and medicate me.

"As you can imagine, there's not a lot to do in a little cell like that, and I quickly became bored. On one occasion when the guard came in for medication, I asked him, 'Could I just please get something to read?' He said, 'Boy, you're not going to get anything to read. They're afraid that you might make a weapon with it to harm one of us or yourself.' I got so angry that I went into an absolute fit and then just passed out on the floor. When I finally awoke, I could see that someone had left a little brown book on the ledge in the door.

"The minute I saw it, I knew what it was. Believe me that book was the last thing I wanted. I didn't think it held any hope for me. I thought I had gone too far and done too much bad stuff. But I retrieved it and opened it. The words jumped out at me: 'God loves you.' Do you know how long it had been since I had heard anyone say they loved me? I didn't think anybody could love me. I knew I had burned all my bridges. But, yet I read, *'For God so loved the world that He gave His only begotten Son, that whoever believes in Him shall not perish, but have eternal life"* (John 3:16).

"I dropped to my knees in that padded cell. Tears began to run down my face. I said, 'God, I've made such a mess out of my life. God, I've hurt so many people and done so many bad things. I don't want to live one more moment the way I've lived the past eighteen years. Jesus, please save me!' Immediately, I felt myself surrounded by one of the brightest lights I'd ever seen. The Spirit of God began to move upon me and God just loved on me.

"Eventually I heard the keys rattle outside the cell, and I knew they had come to give me my sedatives and medication. When they had cuffed me and come into the cell, I told the guard, 'Something happened and I don't think I need this anymore.' He said, 'What's going on? What's happened?' I just held up the Bible and said, 'I've been talking to God.' He didn't believe me and gave me the medication anyway. But in about a week I was able to convince him to just watch me to see if I had truly changed.

"They watched me get better day by day. Within about three weeks they transferred me back to my regular jail cell. When I got off the medication, I asked the guard if I could see the chaplain. I told Chaplain Vance Drummond what had happened to me in that cell, and he said, 'Ronnie, when you cried out to Jesus, He came into your heart. You've been born again, brother; you're a new creation in Christ Jesus.'

"I asked him to please tell me how to keep it, because I had a peace and joy I'd never known before, and I didn't want to lose it. He told me that I should come back every day to his office and to study God's Word with that little Testament and that I should spend time with other believers, and that's just what I did.

"I joined a Bible study and prayer group. When we prayed together, it seemed like the cloud of the Lord would come down upon us. Some of the most glorious times I've ever had in my Christian life took place at the prison in Eastham.

"Three and a half years later, I made parole. I hadn't even been up for parole, so that was an awesome gift from God. In 1991 I was let out of the walls in Huntsville, Texas, a free man. In 1992 God restored my marriage and my relationship with my four children.

"Can the Word of God transform a person's life? Yes! Today I am a Gideon and I am able to go to the jails and prisons with the Word of God and put it into the hands of prisoners."[1]

THE GOSPEL PROCLAIMED BY THOSE "CALLED TO SERVE"

When God calls people to the ministry, He gives them the strength and abilities they will need to carry out His mission for His church. He doesn't necessarily call those who already possess skills and strengths. God provides them as needed in order to secure the success of the mission He has in mind for them.

God called Moses to service at the burning bush as told in Exodus 3. He was told to convince the Pharaoh to let God's people leave Egypt. Moses thought of all kinds of excuses why he was not the man for the job, but the Lord assured Moses that he would be equipped and able to carry out the mission with the power of the Lord. Moses was called to this ministry and God gave him the abilities and skills required to accomplish what God needed done.

Many preachers, teachers, musicians, sportsmen, and businessmen, etc. are given platforms to tell the Good News about Jesus Christ. God prepares them with the skills and opportunities they will need to carry out His plans.

Psalm 139:16 says that God knows all the days of your life before there was one of them—meaning before you were born. He has plans for each of us (Jeremiah 29:11), which for sure includes those He calls to the ministry. Sometimes circumstances are not always completed to human satisfaction. God has a plan for the way things happen as they do. We don't always know the reason why. *"For My thoughts are not your thoughts, Nor are your ways My ways, declares the Lord"* (Isaiah 55:8).

In the following stories several people tell of their call to the ministry and how God prepared them for the call as well as sustained them as they carried out His plan for their lives.

A Soldier for Christ

One day I hitched a ride with my pastor, Dr. Gene Siekmann, from Fort Dodge to Cedar Rapids, Iowa. He was going through Cedar Rapids to the Iowa City Hospital, which was about thirty miles further, to see a church member who recently had surgery. During the drive he told me his story.

Gene was born in southwest Africa, an area now called Namibia. His father was a Lutheran missionary from Barmen, Germany, and had gone to southwest Africa as a single man in 1909. He was required to learn the native language before he could bring his wife-to-be, Paula, to join him. She came about a year later, and they were married in the town of Windhoek.

Their first son, Hans, was born followed by Egon (later changed to Eugene, nickname Gene) in 1912. A baby girl, also named Paula, was born in 1914, but mother Paula died giving birth. Gene's father, Reverend Fredrich Siekmann, was doing travelling mission work in the bush area and didn't learn of his wife's death until he returned home. The baby daughter was kept alive by a native wet nurse, who was also nursing her own baby. Those were difficult, sad and trying times. Pastor Siekmann met another lady from Germany who had come to that area to work. Their friendship evolved into a loving marriage, and three more children were born from this marriage.

In 1922 the Siekmann family moved from southwest Africa back to Germany. Those pre-Hitler times were a struggle. The family could barely support themselves on the small salary Pastor Siekmann was receiving for his part-time work at the Seminary in Barmen, where he had been trained.

What seemed like a hopeless tragedy at the time, resulted in some good news. They later realized this was God's plan for their lives.

They heard that many couples in Holland were willing to accept a German child into their homes for about six weeks. They would feed the children and then send them back with food for their family. Hans (later called John) would not go, but Egon (Gene) was willing to go, along with a train car full of other German children. They went to Meppel, Holland.

A couple was at the station to pick up each child. Gene, now ten years old, had mixed emotions, but looked forward to the good meals. He went to school along with the Dutch children and found that their language, though some different from German, was quite understandable for him. When six weeks ended neither side of this arrangement really wanted to terminate it.

As a result, Gene stayed for a whole year and then rejoined his family in Barmen. His father had written a letter saying that the family was going to be sponsored by his wife's three brothers to travel to the United States. The brothers had previously emigrated from Germany to America.

The family sailed to New York. Upon arrival they were then ushered to Ellis Island. They thought it would only be a day or so before they could continue their trip to Nebraska where their sponsors lived. The family planned to stay there until Pastor Siekmann could find a job in a German-speaking church.

There were very strict rules on Ellis Island. Those in charge tried to find minimal reasons to send people back from where they came. One of the Siekmann children walked in her sleep, another had a simple malady like a cold. Whatever the issue was, the authorities kept the family there for six weeks.

The females were separated from the males in the family. That was hard to explain to the children who needed the understanding and support of both parents. Ultimately they were released and were finally on the train headed for Columbus, Nebraska.

Gene's father now needed to find a German-speaking church, and it just happened (God's providence) there was an area meeting of Presbyterians being held in Columbus at that time. During the meeting it was announced that the German Presbyterian Church in Rensille, Minnesota, was seeking a pastor who could preach in German. Pastor Siekmann applied for the position and was selected. Several years later, after he learned more English, the family moved to a country Presbyterian Church near Lennox, South Dakota, where both English and German were being spoken.

Because they were now Presbyterians instead of Lutherans, Gene applied at the Presbyterian college in Dubuque, Iowa, and received both a work scholarship and a sports scholarship. After graduation he took masters courses at the University of Iowa. His first teaching job was in Denver, a small town near Waterloo, Iowa.

There he taught subjects in his major field of science, as well as German. While there he also did some coaching. Two years later he took a teaching job in Naperville, Illinois. After a few years there, the President of the University of Dubuque contacted him and offered him the position of Director of Admissions, which he accepted.

World War II was rearing its ugly head at this time, and Gene felt he wanted to serve the country he had learned to love and appreciate. He left his position in Dubuque to join the Army. President Dale Welch assured him the university would use an

How God Works in Today's World

interim in his place and his job would be there for him when he returned.

He went into the service and was stationed at Camp Richie, Maryland, located just outside of Washington, D.C. Before being shipped overseas, he was given a three-day pass. He hitchhiked to the nation's capital and planned to go to the USO, (United Service Organization). The USO was founded in 1941 and provided morale and emotional support to members of the U. S. military. During World War II, the USO became the G.I.'s home away from home. Thus began a tradition of entertaining the troops that continues today.

It was raining, and to get out of the weather, Gene ducked into the doorway of New York Avenue Presbyterian Church. Again God intervened in his life. He was not intending to go into the church; he was just escaping the weather on the way to the USO. Gene felt the large hand of Peter Marshall on his shoulder. Peter Marshall was pastor of the church and also Chaplain of the US Senate. Catherine Marshall continues the story in her book, *A Man Called Peter.*

"A soldier, who was stationed at Camp Ritchie, Maryland, hitchhiked to Washington while on a three-day pass. On a rainy Sunday he wandered into New York Avenue Church." The soldier was Gene Siekmann.

"'It was for me, a period of particular *spiritual darkness,*' the soldier said later. 'That Sunday morning God wakened me through Peter Marshall. There was in him a serenity and Christian charm that gripped me and strangely blessed me . . . He was a man of men . . . I thanked Dr. Marshall after the service. He invited me to come to see him in his study the next day, and I did. It ended up by my going home with him to spend the night. We rifled the icebox and talked earnestly into the early morning hours.'"

"This boy later decided to enter the ministry". 'That decision,' he said later, 'dated back to the terrific spiritual impact Peter Marshall had on me that never-to be-forgotten night...'"[1]

Gene said Peter Marshall wrote him several times while he was in the service in Australia, New Guinea, and Japan. Peter Marshal died in 1949. Catherine, Peter's wife, wrote Gene a couple of times and sent Gene a small package which contained a copy of the book *A Man Called Peter* and Peter's billfold, which had his name engraved on it. Gene still has them and treasures them, but says the influence of Peter Marshall on his life is the most treasured.

After three years in the service, Gene returned home to his job at the University of Dubuque. He had met his future wife, Sally, there before going to war. They were married upon his return. Both of their fathers were pastors and both officiated at the wedding. At this writing they have been married sixty-four years and are blessed with two daughters and two sons.

After his experiences in the South Pacific, Gene felt the divine urging to go into the ministry. While a seminary student, he served the Presbyterian Church in Aplington, Iowa, and continued there for five years after graduation. He returned to the University of Dubuque to be Assistant to the President, which evolved into Vice President of Advancement.

After seven years in that position, Gene felt it was time to get back into the ministry. He was called to Marshall, Minnesota, and later to Fort Dodge, Iowa. This is where I met Gene, when he was the minister there at First Presbyterian Church. He baptized both of our children. His wife, Sally, directed choirs in most of his pastorate locations, as well as taught music in high schools.

Even after retirement he served an interim time at a church in Brainerd, Minnesota for a year and a half. His story still does not end there.

After a visit and eventual move to Sun City, Arizona, God opened another door for Gene. A new, large church in Sun City was looking for two associate pastors. The Siekmann's daughter, Paula, was a recent graduate of Fuller Seminary. She and her husband planned to move to Phoenix, where her husband had grown up. God led both Gene and Paula to become associates on the church's staff. Additionally, Sally Siekmann became a part of the church's music ministry, playing for two to three services each Sunday and involved in mid-week music in various ways. All three served together at that same church, Faith Presbyterian in Sun City! Gene celebrated his 99th birthday in 2011!

SCIENCE AND FAITH ARE ALLIES

(Ed. Note: In 1999 I had a heart attack. While in rehab I started listening to Dr. Hugh Ross' radio program, *Reasons to Believe*. Through the years I have followed Dr. Ross on television and enjoyed his many interviews. He has a very interesting life story.)

Reasons To Believe endeavors to show that science and faith are, and always will be, allies, not enemies.[1] Dr. Hugh Ross, founder, scientist, author, teacher and scholar of the Bible and its teachings tells his story.[2]

"Astronomy fascinates me. I started studying it at age seven when I visited the library to find out why stars are hot. Once I found the answer to that question I continued reading every physics and astronomy book I could get my hands on. With my dad's help and the money I saved from collecting pop bottles, I built my first telescope at age sixteen.

"That's the year I turned my attention to cosmology, the origin and structure of the universe. I saw that the big bang was emerging as the most plausible explanation for the history of the universe, and because the big bang implies a cosmic beginning, it also implies a Beginner, a Causal Agent outside or beyond the universe. Thus, I became convinced that belief in God was reasonable, but the immensity of the cosmos made me doubt that a Creator of such awesome magnitude had communicated—in words—to mere humans on this tiny speck called Earth.

"It occurred to me, however, that if this Being had communicated through language, the message would be as clear and consistent and inviting as the universe itself. My curiosity about this cosmic Beginner was now engaged. Armed with knowledge from studies in science and history, I began an investigation of the world's so-called holy books. I reasoned that if men invent a religion, its teachings would reflect human perspectives and, of course, human error. But if the writing were free of such limitations and errors, it must have come from a supernatural source.

Studying Sacred Texts

"At age seventeen, while beginning to serve as director of observations for Vancouver's Royal Astronomical Society, I also began a very private study of the world's sacred texts, testing them for accuracy. My non-religious upbringing freed me from emotional attachment to any particular book or set of beliefs. So I started with the books revered by my neighbors, Eastern religious texts, and worked my way westward.

"One by one each book failed the factuality test, and I gained confidence that my initial skepticism would be affirmed—*until* I picked up and dusted off the Bible that the Gideons had given me several years earlier as part of their distribution program in the public schools. From page one, this book proved an exception. Not only did it provide hundreds of statements that could be tested for accuracy, it also anticipated—thousands of years in advance—many facts of socio-political history and of nature that research would one day confirm. For example, it anticipated the history and current tensions in the Middle East. It also described the four fundamental features of big bang cosmology: 1) the beginning of space and time coincident with the beginning of matter and energy; 2) continual expansion of the universe from the cosmic beginning; 3) the constancy of physical laws; and 4) the pervasiveness of entropy (decay).

"Through nearly two years of study this book's predictive power persuaded me that it must have been inspired by One who knows and guides the past, present, and future.

I had essentially proven to myself that the Bible is more reliable than the laws of physics I focused on in my university courses. The only reasonable conclusion I could see was that the Bible must be the inspired Word of God.

Making a Decision

"However, I delayed making a personal commitment of my life to Christ. Although I knew God with my mind, I struggled to surrender my will to him. What if God changed the direction of my life? What if the people around me found out about my new beliefs? As I continued to wrestle with the decision, my grades began to drop, and I discovered the meaning of Romans 1:21, which warns that rejecting God's truth results in a darkening of the mind. After two months of vacillation, I finally turned my whole self to God and signed the "decision statement" at the back of my now well-worn Bible, acknowledging my life now belonged to Jesus Christ, my Creator and Savior.

"With the help of a provincial scholarship and a National Research Council (NRC) of Canada fellowship, I went on to complete my undergraduate degree in physics at the University of British Columbia and my graduate degrees in astronomy at the University of Toronto.

Growing in Faith

"Through those years I experienced the joy of sharing my faith with several of my fellow students. When the NRC eventually sent me to the United States for postdoctoral research at the California

Institute of Technology, I finally met other sincere followers of Christ.

"The first was Dr. Dave Rogstad, a Christian and a physicist. Dave invited me to Bible studies, introduced me to other believers (including my future wife, Kathy), and challenged me to tell my story and share my faith-building research not only with the non-believers around me but also fellow Christians.

Reasons to Believe

"Encouraged by their response, I began to accept invitations to speak and write about how the growing body of scientific evidence supported belief in Scripture, including its account of creation. In 1986, Kathy and I founded a science apologetics ministry, Reasons to Believe (RTB). We started with a staff of three, one computer, and a tiny office at the back of our church in Sierra Madre, California. But with a lot of prayer and absolute dependence on God, RTB has grown. Twenty-five years later, with more than 25 staff members and thousands of volunteers across the globe, our mission remains the same: to spread the Christian Gospel by demonstrating to both skeptics and believers that sound reason and scientific research consistently support, rather than erode, confidence in the truth of the Bible and faith in the personal, transcendent God revealed in both Scripture and nature.

"Discoveries in astronomy first alerted me to the existence of God, and to this day the Bible's unfathomable depths, predictive power, and remarkable applicability to life rank as major reasons for my faith. I never tire of sharing this news with others or of seeing the joy that shines from the face of someone who has just opened his or her heart to new life in Jesus Christ."

God has given a world-wide platform to this astronomer through television, radio, books and the internet. "At age 17, Dr. Hugh Ross became the youngest person yet to serve as director of observations for Vancouver's Royal Astronomical Society. Between writing dozens of books and articles and founding the Reasons to Believe website, Dr. Ross travels the world challenging high school and university audiences, churches and professional groups to consider what they believe and why."[3]

God reaches millions through Hugh Ross and his witness. For further information, refer to the website: www.reasons.org/.

GOD EMPOWERS THOSE HE CALLS

Dr. Ralph Ehren is an elder in my Church. He is a retired pastor and currently teaches a men's Bible study group. Ralph e-mailed his story to me.[1]

"My dad emigrated from Germany to America in 1912 and settled in Houston, Texas. My mother was born in Iowa and the family of fourteen eventually moved to Houston. This is where my parents met. They married in 1925 and subsequently moved to deep southern Texas in 1930, where my twin brother and I were born.

"During the days of the depression and the dustbowl days of the 1930's our family moved back to Houston where dad took a job as a driller for a water developer. In 1942 we moved again. This time it was to Booneville, Arkansas.

"I didn't know it at the time but God was preparing me. In my early teen years I enrolled in a program sponsored by the Bible Memory Association in Shreveport, Louisiana. I memorized about twenty verses of Scripture each week for twelve weeks in the spring each of the next five years. During those years I memorized about 1,250 Bible verses. This program, unbeknownst to me, became my foundation for the ministry.

"From there I stepped onto the college campus at what today is the University of the Ozarks majoring in history, thinking I would be a teacher for the rest of my life. My college experience was interrupted by two years in the military. I returned to the University of the Ozarks and graduated in 1955. One of the most significant steps along my journey was meeting Betty, who would become my wife. She has been by my side for the past fifty-six plus years. I began a teaching career that I thought would last me a lifetime. The Lord had other plans.

"One evening after church services my pastor asked me, 'Ralph, are you sure the Lord is not calling you to be a preacher?' I had never had that thought in my life and dismissed it as readily as he had suggested it. But over the next year and a half, my subconscious began to work on me until this became a real possibility. However, my wife did not marry a preacher, and so I was not real sure how she would respond to my inclinations. When I could no longer delay the matter, I told her what was going on in my heart and mind. Her response, 'I have wondered when you would recognize this calling!'

"One of the great blessings along the journey of my life was study time at Southwestern Baptist Theological Seminary in Fort Worth, Texas. Since I had never thought of Christian ministry as a life vocation, I had not considered the preparation necessary for such a career. Yet, if I was to be a minister of the Gospel, I was encouraged to study at a Seminary. Betty was more than supportive. She worked as a Media Specialist in the public schools while I went to class.

"While at the Seminary, I became pastor of a small church not far from the Seminary. During my time at this church I learned a lot. After six years of study, I graduated from the Seminary. It was time to move out into the world and apply what I had learned. It was another of God's rich blessings along my life's journey.

I assumed my first full-time pastorate in Laramie, Wyoming. Working with people in Wyoming was much different from anything I had experienced. I had never been in Wyoming. Many of our relatives thought we could have settled in China and been closer to home.

"I had not been there long when there was a knock at the office door. Opening the door, I was face to face with a young man whom I had never seen. He identified himself as an insurance salesman. I might say he was very persuasive. I conceded that insurance was a good investment. However, I convinced him that I could not fit the cost into my budget, so this essential would have to be put on hold.

"Then our visit took an entirely new direction. Reflecting upon this visit some months later, I became convinced his appearance was motivated by the Lord Himself. As is evident by the following, this young atheist became one of my best friends in several ways. It was obvious that as much as I might need and even want to buy insurance, I could not afford it. It became equally evident he had another motive for being there.

"This young man asked the question: 'I notice by the sign on the front of the building that this is a Baptist Church. I know that Baptists don't drink, smoke, dance or cuss. What do you do?' It was a serious question! Little did I know where this question would lead.

"He told me much about himself. I needed to respond to him. He had literally grown up on the sidewalks of New York. He said he had never been inside a church of any kind until he was in the military service. And the only reason he went then was because that's what his buddies did on Sunday. So rather than stay by himself he went with them. He had no ideas at all about church, its meaning or its mission. But he was curious and I was glad to help. We visited for about four hours that afternoon.

"The next Sunday he was in church with his wife and four small, well-behaved children. They sat in the second pew. On Monday morning my friend came by the office to ask me questions about the previous morning's message. I was very impressed with his obvious attention in the service as he quoted me almost verbatim over and over asking 'what did you mean by these statements?' I patiently discussed each of his concerns.

"The next day he was back again. He surely had been thinking about what he had heard but had not understood. So we talked again. On Wednesday he was in my office again pursuing the meaning of my sermon . . . and again on Thursday. The next Sunday he and his family were again in their pew near the front of the Sanctuary. He listened intently. I know he did because the next morning he was in my office again asking me more questions about what I had said. He had a tremendous memory and quoted me repeatedly. I was impressed with his interest and ability.

"This pattern repeated itself for the next twelve months. Let me say, I had promised the Lord that I would be faithful to His Word as I understood it so long as I preached. I also became quickly aware that I needed to be very careful in *speaking for the Lord* because I would be challenged and have to explain myself regularly. My friend was never belligerent or argumentative, only curious. It was rather easy to talk with him because from the very beginning he seemed genuinely interested in what he was hearing.

"About six months into sermonizing each week, I preached a sermon on the topic of heaven and eternal life. I planned to speak on the subject of hell and judgment the following week. True-to-form, my friend dropped by early Monday morning. He asked, 'Do you really believe what you said in your sermon yesterday?' I replied, 'Yes, when I am in the pulpit I do not speak for myself but for the Lord, and I try to be as careful as I can to reflect His mind to the people.'

"His response was, 'You seem to have a reasonable amount of intelligence, but I don't see how anyone could believe what you were saying.' I asked, 'What do you think happens to a person when he dies?' Response: 'Oh, it's like going to sleep. You just drift off into unconsciousness and never wake up.' Then I asked, 'Have you ever died?' With a funny look on his face he said, 'Not that I know of.' So I showed him that his conclusion was one of faith not fact. He did not know what he believed to be a fact; he only believed what he thought he knew. As you might guess, this led to a lengthy and interesting conversation.

"I'm grateful that this atheist, who became my friend, was placed in my path early in my ministry. He taught me many good lessons that have served me well throughout my ministry. One of the most valuable lessons I learned was the fact that at least some people do listen to the sermon. My responsibility to the Lord coupled with the fact that some are listening impressed upon me the necessity of diligent preparation and much prayer. Furthermore, the eternal destiny of some people rests upon their hearing a word from the Lord about the facts of life. And, I was His spokesman. This is an awesome and very serious responsibility.

"I subsequently became pastor in Casper, Wyoming. My friend often found himself in Casper on business, and he would frequently come by. Many times we would have coffee and visit. On one such visit, he told he was going to get drunk that night. I said, 'Do you not remember how sick you get when you drink?' My response was based on earlier experiences when he would be bed-ridden in total seclusion for about four days when he had over-imbibed. His response to my question was 'Yes, but think of the fun I am going to have before I get sick!!'

"Throwing his words back at him, I said, 'That's sick. You seem to have a reasonable amount of intelligence, but I don't know how any person in his right mind can do to himself what you say you will do knowing what happens.' He just smiled!

"My friend and I got up from the table. We shook hands and walked out the door and parted ways. I never saw him again. I have often wondered about him, where he is, what he is doing. Most of all I wondered if the seed that had been planted in his heart took root. Maybe the seed took root in the hearts of his family—I just don't know.

"What I do know is that has God promised: *'So will My word be which goes forth from My mouth; it will not return to Me empty, without accomplishing what I desire, and without succeeding in the matter for which I sent it"* (Isaiah 55:11).

"Another experience I remember during my pastorate happened in Laramie, a mere three weeks after we arrived. One of the faithful ladies in the church made an appointment to visit with her new Pastor. She was there on time. I was happy and anxious to get acquainted with those in leadership responsibilities in the church.

"However, this visit became more puzzling and challenging after it had been concluded. During the time she sat in my office, she boldly announced that 'the Lord directs this church through me!' She indicated that anytime I had issues to be dealt with, questions about anything related to the church, I was simply to call her and she would handle the matter. I didn't think she was serious. But, with the passing of time I learned she was.

"How does a new Pastor handle an issue like this? I could not go to her, she was the issue. I gave much thought and prayer time to this matter. I finally decided that I must talk with the Deacons to see if I had misunderstood her. So I made appointments with each of the Deacons to meet them in their homes to discuss the matter. This took several weeks, but I finally saw all of them along with their wives. Then, I called the Deacons together at the Church. I reminded them that I had seen each of them along with their wives in their homes. I asked, 'Is my evaluation of the situation correct?'

"To a man they agreed this was a serious problem because of her commitment to her own stated position. It had been a problem long before I arrived on the scene, but nothing had been done about it. Then, I asked, 'What should be done about this issue?' They responded with complete silence, indicating that nothing would be done. Heretofore, they had been able to work around the problem, so the Pastor would be left to do the best he could, but on his own. They would not become involved.

"In the ensuing weeks the matter became more harassing. I was away at a revival meeting. While I was gone, she called my wife all hours of the day and night, not to talk but to inform her how things were and were going to be at the church. She never accused me of any wrongdoing other than the fact that I had not consulted her on matters she felt were her responsibility. We had an eighteen month old daughter at the time and my wife did not need her harassment.

"Not many months into the year, the wife of a fellow pastor, some miles from Laramie, died. Almost immediately the lady announced that the Lord had instructed her to abandon her husband and four children to become the new wife of the bereaved pastor.

"She drove to his house to announce the Lord's plans for him. Then she returned home to make all the arrangements to take up residence with him. In the few days between, the grieving pastor packed his belongings and left the area. He did not want her to find him, so he resigned and left the area without a forwarding address.

"The presence and demeanor of this lady was far more distressing than anything she did. I believed she was demon-possessed, but that is not easily identifiable. It is more clearly discernible (through the Holy Spirit) in relationship with such a person.

"*But a natural man does not accept the things of the Spirit of God, for they are foolishness to him, and he cannot understand them, because they are spiritually appraised*" (I Corinthians 2:14).

"God called me, trained and led me. Even now, after more than a dozen moves and having served Him as both a teacher and pastor, and though I'm in my 80s, God still opens doors for me to teach His Gospel."

HAND GRENADE EXPLODES, LEADS TO A MINISTRY

Dave Roever[1] grew up in a loving family in South Texas. He never thought he would go to war. Then he received his draft notice at the height of the Vietnam War. He joined the Navy and became part of the Brown Water Black Beret, serving as a riverboat gunner in Vietnam.

After just eight months of duty Dave was badly burned, nearly beyond recognition. A phosphorous grenade he was about to throw exploded in his hand. He was hospitalized for fourteen months and had several major surgeries. The fact that he survived and is alive today is miraculous.

He was so disfigured that he wasn't sure his wife would love him anymore; but, she stood by him. Dave is still severely disfigured. Yet, he has become an internationally known speaker and a gifted communicator with a humorous style. His worldwide travels take him to a variety of settings. He speaks at public schools, military installations, businessmen's meetings and youth conventions, among others. Roever (pronounced Reever) has been a frequent guest on national television talk shows.

Everywhere Dave goes, he carries a message of hope. He shares how he experienced loneliness and talks about his disfigurement and pain. He is very qualified to speak to troops who have been injured in the military, because he was in war, too. Like many of them, he served, was injured and had to suffer much pain as he went through the recovery process. He offers messages with concrete solutions for life's problems, and he also talks about triumphs that life gives. The foundation for Dave's faith is hope, and he is sustained by the love and support of his family.

The Department of the Navy awarded Dave the Purple Heart, thirty-four years after his injury. Dave was also awarded an honorary doctor degree in May, 2005. It was given in recognition of his exceptional life and outstanding service.

In December, 2004, Dave secured property in the beautiful Wet Mountains facing the Sangre de Cristo Mountains near Westcliffe, Colorado. He and his wife, Brenda, have built a training center they called Eagle's Summit Ranch. This facility is for those who have been seriously wounded in the war on terror and are in need of emotional reconstruction.[2]

The hope is to restore and encourage these badly injured military men and train them to know how to turn the tragic things that have happened to them into triumph. Dave wants to show a hurting world how Christ can make a difference in life. These wounded American warriors are equipped with the courage to go before an audience and share the story about their military experience and tell how they survived.

He explains, "Hundreds of our treasured defenders of freedom are left wounded and in despair. Medical intervention puts these wounded warriors back on their feet with artificial limbs, but it cannot place them back on their feet spiritually. At Eagle's Summit Ranch the goal is to glue them back together emotionally and spiritually."[3]

Billy Graham has said, "Dave Roever has had a wonderful ministry with young people and military installations in conjunction with our crusades. God has obviously given him the gift of an evangelist, and I am grateful for his ministry of sharing the Gospel."[4]

Roever is a true testimonial to the Bible verse: *"I can do all things through Him who strengthens me"* (Philippians 4:13).

PROPHET OF PROPHECY

According to his web site, Hal Lindsey was once a self-confessed "devout pagan."[1] In the early 1950s he was living the fast-life, and worked hard as a riverboat captain on the Mississippi River in New Orleans. He had attended church in his youth, had even been baptized.

He drifted away from his faith because he found no one who could provide guidance and teach him what it meant to be a Christian. Then, in 1955, something happened that got him thinking about God again. It was a very foggy night, and he needed to get his boat across the busy Mississippi River. That's when God stepped in.

His boat was not equipped with radar or a signal alarm. He was like a blind person sailing into the unknown. Hal was near the middle of the river, when it felt like an *unseen hand* caused him to suddenly turn the vessel hard right. It was then he realized that he had almost collided with a large steamship. There was no doubt in his mind that the hand of God had shielded him from a catastrophic collision with the other vessel.

The incident made Hal rethink how he was living his life. He found a Gideon's New Testament that he had kept since he was young, and he began to read it. He had kept this small Bible in his duffle bag as a kind of good luck charm. As he began to read, there still were questions he couldn't answer and things he couldn't understand.

Then Hal met a man known as the "crazy preacher" down at the docks. The man was actually a devout Christian, who had recently come to the waterfront. At last Hal found someone who could help him understand the Bible and answer the questions he had and help him to grown in his Christian faith! Hal became a born-again Christian!

He went on to graduate from Dallas Theological Seminary and worked with Campus Crusade for Christ for eight years. He served as the pastor of Tetelestai Christian Center in Torrance, California, and was awarded a Doctorate from the California School of Theology in 1994.[2]

Hal Lindsey is best known for his many books on Bible prophecy and the End Times. Sales of his books worldwide now total more than thirty-six million! The book probably most widely read is *The Late Great Planet Earth.* In it he describes his interpretation of the End Times. It was first published in 1970 by Zondervan and it became the best-selling non-fiction book of the 1970s. Some have called Hal Lindsey "The Jeremiah of Today."[3]

Other books he has written are: *Satan is Alive and Well on Planet Earth, The Liberation of Planet Earth, There's a New World Coming, 1980's—Countdown to Armageddon, The Final Battle, The Terminal Generation, Planet Earth: the Final Chapter, The Rapture, Planet Earth—2000 A. D., Apocalypse Code, Blood Moon, Vanished into Thin Air,* and *The Everlasting Hatred: The Roots of Jihad.*[4]

Some criticize him and say that his predictions of Christ's Second Coming have not been fulfilled. They forget that even Jesus said no one will know exactly when the End will come. *"But of that day and hour no one knows, not even the angels of heaven, nor the Son, but the Father alone"* (Mathew 24:36).

Psalm 90:4 says, *"For a thousand years in Your sight are like yesterday when it passes by, or as a watch in the night."* In 2 Peter 3:8 it states, *"But do not let his one fact escape your notice, beloved, that with the Lord one day is like a thousand years, and a thousand years like one day."* Additionally, Christ did say that there will be signs that point to His imminent return. Many Christians feel that the time of our Lord's return is drawing near. The fulfillment of God's prophecies is becoming evident at a faster pace than ever before.

The Hal Lindsey Report, a weekly report about how current events are fulfilling Bible prophesy, can be seen on various television stations. Further information on his ministry and his interpretation of current events, as they relate to biblical prophecy and the End Times, are available on his web site: www.hallindsey.com/.

HE PROVED JESUS IS TRUE

Josh McDowell was the son of a "town drunk".[1] Due to his father's abuse and alcoholism, young Josh was bitter towards life and had a very low self esteem. He hated his father, who beat his mother and gave Josh no love or attention. He felt Christianity was worthless. Yet, at last count, since 1960 Josh McDowell has written or co-authored over 120 books supporting Christianity.[2] This is Josh's story.

When Josh entered Kellogg Community College in Battle Creek, Michigan, he intended to pursue a legal career. He claimed he was an avowed agnostic. He ridiculed Christians and thought little of their beliefs, which he considered completely unbelievable.

A professor and fellow classmates in one of his classes challenged him to try and disprove Christianity. He took on the challenge and set out to prove that Christ's claims of His deity were false and that the historical authenticity of the Bible could not be relied upon nor confirmed as accurate. He planned to use research to discredit the claims of Jesus Christ. He planned to put in writing the facts that would, once and for all, prove that Christianity was a fraud.

But, the more he studied, the more he couldn't ignore the facts he discovered. He found indisputable evidence that the claims and beliefs of Christians were true. He realized that the Bible was the most historically reliable document of all antiquity, and that Christ's claim that he was God was for real.

One night Josh was not able to sleep. He couldn't keep from thinking about Jesus. Finally he knelt to pray and asked Jesus to come into his heart and accepted Him as his Lord. After his conversion, Josh's plans for law school turned instead to plans to spread the truth about Jesus Christ to a world that doubted it just like he had. Josh completed his college degree at Wheaton College and then attended Talbot Theological Seminary, where he graduated Magna Cum Laude with a Master of Divinity degree.

Josh had cut all contacts with his father. When he accepted Christ as his Savior, a powerful love consumed his life. He described how it affected his feelings for his father: "God's love took that hatred, turned it upside down, and emptied it out. I looked my father in the eyes and said, 'Dad, I love you,' and I really meant it."[3]

A short time later, his dad visited him. "It was one of his few sober days," Josh said. "Dad paced nervously around the room and finally blurted out, 'Son, how can you love a father like me?' Josh answered, "Dad, six months ago I despised you." He shared the story of his research and conclusions that Jesus Christ was the Son of God and confessed, "I have placed my trust in Christ, received God's forgiveness, and invited Him into my life. He has changed me. God has taken away my hatred, and now I love and accept you just the way you are."[4]

After they talked for almost an hour, Josh's dad said, "Son, if God can do in my life what I've seen Him do in yours, then I want to trust Him as my Savior and Lord." His father's life changed completely and immediately. Josh says his father was tempted to drink alcohol once after that, but threw it away before he took a sip.[5]

Campus Crusade for Christ and particularly the Josh McDowell Ministry reaches young people as they teach about the truth and love of Jesus worldwide. Josh has devoted his life to telling the world about Jesus Christ. He is well known as a compelling and convincing speaker and has talked to more than ten million young people around the globe.[6]

One of the most well-known books Josh has written is *The New Evidence that Demands a Verdict.* It is a very comprehensive book on apologetics (defense of Christianity and why the Bible is true). It has been named one of the twentieth century's top forty books and one of the thirteen most influential books of the last fifty years on Christian thought by *World Magazine.* More than fifteen million copies of his book *More Than a Carpenter* have been printed and is available in eighty-five languages.[7]

Josh and his son, Sean, have co-authored several books, one of which is about Easter. It is called *Evidence for the Resurrection: What It Means for Your Relationship with God.* Released in February, 2009, it was written with the hopes of providing pastors and youth ministers with a way to teach the true, historical meaning of Easter, as an alternative to a holiday focused on bunnies and candy.[8]

Presently the Josh McDowell Ministry headquarters is located in Plano, Texas. Affiliate offices are located around the country. Further information on Josh McDowell and his ministry may be found at: www.josh.org.

MISSIONARIES SLAIN, WIVES CONTINUE MINISTRY

This is the story of the missionary ministry of Martin and Gracia Burnham.[1] In 1986 Gracia and Martin Burnham began work as missionaries with the New Tribes Mission in the Philippines. For seventeen years Martin flew as a jungle pilot. He delivered mail, supplies and provided encouragement to other missionaries. He also transported sick and injured patients to medical centers. Gracia supported his efforts and home-schooled their children, all of whom were born in the Philippines.

In 2001 the Burnhams celebrated their eighteenth wedding anniversary at the Dos Palmas Resort on Palawan Island. It was there, on May 27, that they and several other guests were kidnapped by the Abu Sayyaf Group, a Muslim militant group linked to Al-Qaeda. They were taken to an ASG stronghold on Basilan Island. The ASG militants were unfamiliar with the Koran and had only a sketchy notion of Islam. They considered it as a set of behavioral rules to be violated when it suited them. Kidnapping, murder and theft were justified by their special status as holy warriors.

In the ensuing months some of the hostages were killed, and most were ransomed and set free. The militants demanded a $1 million ransom for the Burnhams. They were paid $330,000, but still refused to release them. By November, 2001, only Gracia, Martin and one other hostage remained in captivity. For the next 376 day the militants kept on the move. Their captives had to travel with them, facing near starvation and unrelenting fatigue. Days of boredom were mixed with unexpected gun battles between ASG and the Philippine military. Often they were in the crossfire and witnessed many cold-blooded murders.

Through it all the Burnhams held onto their faith, often encouraging one another by recalling and reciting all of the Bible verses they could remember, like:

> *"I love you with an everlasting love"* (Jeremiah 31:3) and
> *"If God is for us, who is against us?"* (Romans 8:31b).

Gracia watched as Martin lived out his faith. He told her that they had to remember what was true, and that God's Word was the truth. Martin's attitude expressed the heart of a servant and surely served as a testimony to her, as well as their captors.

They named one of their kidnappers "57" because he always carried a large AK 57 rifle. When Musab told them he could not read the Koran, Gracia suggested he should have the Koran translated into his language. He said, "Oh no, then the Koran would be corrupted."

Musab "57" suffered from headaches, and the Burnham's treated him with some medications they had. They could have just done nothing and let "57" suffer. Martin's guiding principle was to try and make enemies into brothers, remembering what Jesus said from the cross when he was crucified: *"Father, forgive them for they know not what they do"* (Luke 23:24). Martin and Gracia planted seeds of love. Instead of feeling hate toward their kidnappers, they felt compassion for their ignorance.

Martin and the other hostage were killed on June 7, 2002, in a firefight between the Philippine military and the Abu Sayyaf Group. Gracia was wounded in the leg, but was freed. She returned to the United States and to her children.

For the next year she wrote a book about her experience. This book was called *In the Presence of My Enemies*, and tells the details about the captive experience. She has also written *To Fly Again: Surviving the Tailspins of Life*. God gave her a platform to speak to the world.

Gracia established The Martin and Gracia Burnham Foundation. She hopes to provide funds and resources to support the following:

> Ministry to Muslims   Tribal Mission
> Missionary Aviation   The Persecuted Church

The foundation is administered through the Servant Christian Community Foundation. Additional information is found on the website: www.graciaburnham.org/.

Similar to the above is the story of the missionary ministry of Jim and Elisabeth Elliot.[2] Jim and Elisabeth Elliot met while attending Wheaton College. They were married in Quito, Ecuador in 1953. Jim wanted to be a missionary to the unreached people of the world and knew that the Auca (alternatively known as Huaorani) in eastern Ecuador were in that category. The Auca were very fierce, and no one had yet succeeded in making contact with them and come out alive.

After discovering the whereabouts of the Auca in 1956, Jim and four other missionaries went into Auca territory. Jim Elliot, Nate Saint, and Ed McCully had met in college and shared a burning desire to follow Jesus' command, *"Go into all the world and preach the gospel to all creation"* (Mark 16:15).

Missionary Roger Youderiano had been working in Ecuador with the Jivaros tribe of head-shrinkers, and was a paratrooper trained in World War II. The fifth person in their group was a friend of Jim and Ed's named Pete Fleming.

For years they had prayed for this primitive group who had never heard the redemption story of peace with God through the death and resurrection of Christ. Oil prospectors were coming closer and closer to the Huao natives. The men felt they should act soon so they would not lose the opportunity for peaceful contact.

They had a seemingly friendly contact with three of the tribe members, but were then speared to death while attempting to evangelize them. A movie called *End of the Spear* was later made to tell their story.

God took these common young men of uncommon commitment and used them for His own glory. They were killed and never had the privilege to tell the Huaorani of the God they loved and served. Jim Elliot is remembered for this statement from his journal, "He is no fool who gives what he cannot keep to gain that which he cannot lose."[3]

Jim and Elisabeth's daughter was just ten months old when her father died. After her husband's death, Elisabeth remained in Ecuador and continued work with the Quichua Indians. No doubt by God's plan, she met two Auca women who lived with her for a year. They proved to be the key that opened the door to the Auca, allowing her to live for two years among the same tribe who had killed her husband! After these two years, she returned to her missionary work with the Quichua, ministering to them until 1963, when she and her daughter returned to the States.

Since then she has written many books and has toured the country well into her 70s speaking about her thoughts and experiences. Among her books are *Shadow of the Almighty: The Life and Testament of Jim Elliot* and *Through Gates of Splendor*.[4]

For every unreached person who is taught about God and salvation by such dedicated people like Martin Burham and Jim Eliot, there are thousands more who need to be reached. Because of the courage and strong faith of these missionaries and their wives, others continue to evangelize with even more determination and dedication.

Those they had hoped to meet and teach have been reached, thanks to the groundwork and ultimate sacrifice they made. With His faithfulness, God continues to multiply these successes. It is a memorial to their obedience.

MY WAY WAS NOT GOD'S WAY

The following is an e-mail letter sent by Rev. Dr. Keith Small. He is one of the missionaries our church fellowship class supports. Rev. Dr. Small received his BA degree from Western Michigan University; his Masters in Theology from Dallas Theological Seminary, and his PhD in Islamics through the London School of Theology.

He has "taught undergraduate and postgraduate levels in Britain and internationally concerning Islamics and Christian ministries to Muslims. In addition to his academic credentials he has more than twenty years of ministry experience among Muslims and Christians in Europe."[1]

He made a trip to South Africa to a conference to present a book he had written as well as do some teaching. In his letter he related this story.

"Dear Friends,

"Thank you so much for your prayers and all the encouraging messages while I was in South Africa. It was so good to know you were praying. I am well now and home after quite an adventure.

"The third day of the Congress and the day I was supposed to teach in a Dialogue session (a workshop of sorts), I came down with acute gastro-enteritis. I didn't realize how serious it had become until about 6:00 p.m. when I fainted in my hotel room. I woke up on the floor and promptly called the hotel doctor. He immediately ordered me taken to Christian Barnard Memorial Hospital (site of the world's first heart transplant in the late 1960s). There I was put on fluids and antibiotics, and over the next two days as my symptoms subsided, I regained my strength.

"I was released early Friday evening, and on Saturday I rested in my hotel room. On Sunday, which was the last day of the Congress, I was able to attend the major sessions.

"As you can imagine, the question that was big on my mind was this. Why did God bring me all the way from London to South Africa to the Congress, only to have me miss more than half of it? I still don't know the full answer, but I can say the main goals I had for my involvement were more than met.

"All of the books that I took to give away on CD—about 900—were taken, and people were asking for more of them. From these, one hundred will go into the hands of Christian workers ministering to Muslims in South Africa and all of the Christian training institutions there.

"This is particularly strategic in that for more than thirty years, Muslims from South Africa have been setting the dominant attitudes and arguments that Muslims use around the world against Christianity and the Bible. An additional one hundred CDs were retained for the man who asked me to produce the book for the Congress. They will be given to particular leaders he thinks will find them useful.

"I myself gave out probably a hundred or so to key leaders, workers and teachers training missionaries on at least five continents, and to key Christian educators from the United States, Europe, Egypt, Jordan, and Korea.

"Another blessing was talking with the doctor who attended me. I found out quickly he had an interest in Christian things but was not committed to any particular church. As we got to know each other, he became more interested in my work, and as a thank you I gave him a copy of the book-on-CD. He read the cover, asked me a couple of additional questions about how it compared the Bible to the Qur'an, and then he said seriously, 'I am very interested in this. I will certainly read it!' He also agreed to write me when he is done to let me know what he thought.

"What I was able to experience at the Congress was wonderful. It was a tremendous joy to sit in the congress hall with 4000+ believers from around the world. At my table we had brothers and sisters from Jordan, Zambia, Uganda, the USA, and Korea. I was able to meet many pastors from the Middle East and Africa who minister amongst Muslims. While there I also received invitations to teach in Jordan, Egypt, and South Africa.

"Even though I did not get to teach my session, the paper that I prepared for the Congress will go up on the Lausanne Congress website, so it is available. This will actually make it available to more people than if it had just been presented at the Congress.

"In our weakness, God demonstrates His strength. I went to serve, and even though I was not able to serve quite as I had originally hoped, God more than exceeded my expectations and prayers. Now we will see how He continues to accomplish His will from the many seeds that have been planted."

"For My thoughts are not your thoughts, Nor are your ways My ways," declares the Lord (Isaiah 55:8).

SERVANT OF GOD IN THE MAKING

There is a young man in my church who recently graduated with a Mechanical Engineering Degree from Eastern Michigan University in Ypsilanti, Michigan. The Lord also led him to pursue an internship with Athletes in Action, a ministry of Campus Crusade.

Owen had lived in this same area of Michigan in his younger years. There he, his two brothers, mom and dad attended a local Christian church. His mother was a championship swimmer in high school and college, and he and his brothers pursued the same athletic sports endeavor.

The family moved to Frisco, Texas, when Owen was in grade school. He continued his middle and high school education in the local schools. The family became members of Stonebriar Community Church, where Chuck Swindoll has his preaching ministry.

One of Owen's hobbies was building models of airplanes. He hoped someday to be a pilot and dreamed of attending the United States Naval Academy. Throughout his school years Owen distinguished himself as a swimmer, winning many trophies and awards.

Swimming and school took up much of his week, and Owen found it difficult to participate in mid-week youth activities at church along with all of the practice time needed for swimming. As he approached high school, however, he felt more and more the need to be involved in church activities, Bible study and fellowship with other Christians. So, he made concerted efforts to accomplish this.

As high school graduation approached, it became obvious he was scholarship material both academically and for his swimming prowess. He applied and was accepted for consideration to the United States Naval Academy, only to see this dream dashed when he was unable to pass the ear/hearing portion of the medical exam.

This was a definite change in course for him and a real "sit down and re-think" time. He and his parents researched other college options, looking for a good fit with the degree he wanted along with a sports scholarship to enable him to carry on his swimming career and pay for his education.

He considered many universities and finally chose Eastern Michigan University. Their swimming program fit his skill level, yet offered him an achievable challenge, and also provided him with a full four-year scholarship!

Owen was pleased to know that there were swim-team members who were also committed Christians. As his family had lived previously in the area, he was able to reconnect with his former church home there. Arrangements were made through the pastor for a fellow classmate to give Owen a ride to church every Sunday. It was also providential that the classmate's father was connected with Campus Crusade at the nearby University of Michigan in Ann Arbor, Michigan.

During the summer between his freshman and sophomore years, Owen returned to Texas and served as an intern leader for a junior high camp sponsored by Stonebriar Community Church. He was mentored by a lead counselor. Owen was impressed with the leader's ability to know just where to look in the Bible to help answer questions asked by the young campers. He told the others during the final night share-time that observing this skill of the leader made him realize that he wanted to be able to do that, too.

At the end of the camp, one of the other interns showed Owen a particular Bible verse he had on the background of his phone. The verse was: *"Iron sharpens iron, so one man sharpens another"* (Proverbs 27:17). Owen thanked him, but then more or less forgot about the verse.

One Sunday after he returned to college, he went to the church he had attended the year before. The pastor there, the late Bill Moore (a Dallas Theological Seminary graduate) preached a sermon on that very same verse! Shortly after that Owen signed up to receive daily Bible verses from Facebook, and that same verse was the one displayed! It was at that point Owen knew God was sending him a message. He felt he was being led to further study the Word and to serve the Lord and bring others to Christ.

During the next year Owen met more fellow Christian students and members of the swim team who had committed their lives to the Lord. He was especially struck by the enthusiasm and hunger of newly-saved Christians. They were excited and eager for Bible learning and had many questions. It created a new vitality in Owen's own walk with the Lord, as some came to him seeking answers to their questions.

He became a leader of an athlete Bible study group and saw it grow. He got to know some of the staff of Campus Crusade at nearby University of Michigan. It also has an Athletes in Action organization, which is part of Campus Crusade at many colleges.[1]

When his friend, who was providing the Sunday transportation graduated, another friend introduced him to his church. Owen began going there every Sunday. He was inspired to see other students accept Christ, and Owen soon felt a call to the ministry. After graduating with his degree he applied and was accepted to be an intern for Athletes in Action/Campus Crusade.

He is watching and looking for direction from the Lord to walk where the Lord wants him to go. The chorus of the song by Doris Akers called *Lead Me, Guide Me* goes like this:[2]

> Lead me, guide me along the way,
> For if you lead me I cannot stray.
> Lord let me walk each day with Thee.
> Lead me, oh Lord lead me.

God has led Owen on this journey. May the Lord continue to bless and lead him as he lives his future serving the Lord.

SHIP MINISTRY TEACHES, PREACHES AND SAVES

Today Operation Mobilisation works around the world in over one hundred ten countries with six thousand workers. This ministry of evangelism works to motivate and equip people to share the love of God and to plant churches in areas where Christ is least known.[1] The organization was started in the 1950s by George Verwer.

When he was in high school, George Verwer was given the Gospel of John by one of his teachers, Dorothea Clapp. She had a mission to acquaint young people with God's Word. When he was sixteen years old George became a Christian at a Billy Graham revival in New York, and dedicated his life to the Lord.

After graduation he and two other friends began to travel and distribute Gospels and other Christian literature wherever they went. While traveling in Spain, they soon realized that the task of reaching nonbelievers around the world was overwhelming.

As they shared their desire to distribute the Word world-wide, they found good response from other Christians who wanted to be part of it as well. The idea of *Operation Mobilisation* was born (officially named in 1981). They had a vision of a global mission.

At first, the focus was on Europe. Verwer believed that leadership should come from the local Christian community and not be led by foreigners. In the 1960s the men concentrated on training national leaders to take the Gospel throughout Europe, including what was then Eastern Europe. As they developed teams for the work of global mission, they found that moving the teams around from one country to another was expensive and took a lot of time.

By 1970, when the first Logos ship was purchased, the vision had evolved into using a ship ministry to transport the training teams to various countries. They could dock for extended periods and train local Christians to become leaders in their own country. This proved effective and more economically practical.

Since then their various ships have gone to over five hundred different ports in more than one hundred sixty countries and territories. More than four million visitors have come aboard.

Since 2009 the mission team has sailed with its fourth ship, the 12,519 ton *MV Logos Hope*. Originally built in 1973 as a car ferry, it was refitted for their use. The ship in service prior to *Logos Hope* was called *Logos II*. It had seen over ten million visitors come aboard in more than eighty countries in the two decades it was in service.

The ship sails with a crew of four hundred, all of whom serve as volunteers.[2] They come from over forty different countries. Most are young people who dedicate two years of their lives to this service and raise their own money for support. The members of the ship's crew are also voluntary. This includes the captain. They are trained and qualified as required by international maritime regulations.

The funding for the ship operation comes from three sources:[3] (1) Half comes from the personnel serving on board, raised through funds given by their friends, family and other supporters. (2) A quarter is raised through the sale of books and non-book items (such as souvenirs) at the family book fairs that are held onboard. (3) The last quarter comes from gifts and donations provided by individuals, trusts, foundations, etc.

The book fairs draw many people to the ships. They can select from over five thousand book titles, which appeal to a broad range of ages and interest. They feature many subjects in addition to the Gospel—cooking, sports, science, hobbies, children's books, etc. Grants of books have a huge impact in developing countries, especially when they are provided to schools, libraries, colleges, churches and universities.

As they sail to various ports, the crew sees the needs of the world first-hand. They help by distributing food, medical and other donated supplies, building houses, providing education and training, and giving medical aid. The volunteer crew members lend a listening ear and share the message of the Gospel. They help visitors to the ship get to know God in a personal way. The handling of immediate needs is always there, but they also strive to do what they can to start and foster long-term life-changes in the community. Crew members are richly blessed by the experience and develop a life-time desire to serve the Lord.

As stated on their website: "Our desire is to share the knowledge of God's love and compassion with every visitor to our ships and with the wider community in every port".[4]

This is another way that God is working in today's world to spread the Gospel in order to fulfill Jesus' command as found in Mark 16:15: *"And He said to them, 'Go into all the world and preach the gospel to all creation."*

Additional information on this ministry can be found on the website: www.om.org/

TRANSLATOR OF THE BIBLE FOR MILLIONS

Wycliffe Bible Translators was founded in 1942 by William Cameron Townsend.[1] Prior to that time he had served as a missionary to the Cakchiquel Indians in Guatemala.[2] As he worked with the Indians, Townsend realized that not only could the natives not read the Spanish Bibles he brought with him, but they didn't even have a written form of their own language!

He decided to live among the Cakchiquels so he could learn their complex language. He created an alphabet for it. After analyzing the grammar, he translated the New Testament into their language. It was a remarkable achievement, as he completed this in just ten years!

He became concerned about other minority language groups who also did not have Bibles in their own language and opened Camp Wycliffe in Arkansas in 1934. Here he planned to train people in basic linguistics and translation methods. The camp was named after John Wycliffe, who completed the first European translation of the entire English Bible in 1382.[3]

In the beginning only a few students enrolled in the program at Camp Wycliffe. Their first endeavor was in Mexico, which has continued successfully for many years. From this small beginning it has grown into a worldwide ministry. Currently it includes the Summer Institute of Linguistics (SIL), Wycliffe Bible Translators, Wycliffe Associates, and the technical department of SIL known as JAARS. SIL and Wycliffe Bible Translators have completed more than seven hundred translations with many more in progress.[4]

There are at least a thousand unwritten languages in the world today. It is a seemingly impossible task to reach all peoples of the world with a Bible in their native tongue. The workers at Wycliffe rely on God to make the impossible possible by providing the people and the resources needed. They want to realize Townsend's goal that every man, woman and child be able to read God's Word in his or her own language.

There is still much work to be done.

Statistics from their website in 2010, www.wycliffe.org/About/Statistics.aspx,[5] are as follows:

- The population of the world is 6.5 billion+ people.
- There are 6,800+ languages spoken world-wide today.
- There are 2,000+ languages without any of the Bible, *no* translation yet started.
- There are 340 million people who speak these 2,000+ languages.
- Wycliffe is currently working on 1,500+ other translation programs.
- Nearly 75% of remaining Bible translation needs are located in the three areas of greatest need.
- There are 1,211 language communities which have access to the New Testament in their mother tongue.
- There are 457 language communities which have access to the entire Bible in a language they can understand.

For additional information on this ministry, see www.wycliffe.org/.

God Wanted Him to be a Policeman

Bob Vernon told his story on radio broadcasts of *Focus on the Family*.[1&2] It describes just how much God was involved in the details of his life and career.

At age twelve Bob Vernon became a Christian. As he matured, he prayed and asked God, "What do You want me to do with my life?" Psalm 37:23 says, *"The steps of a man are established by the Lord, and He delights in his way."* Several years passed, and he had not received a specific direction to follow. Then it came time for him to choose a college, and he wasn't sure what do there, either.

One day his mother mentioned Biola University, which would offer a biblically-centered education. It wasn't long before his sister also mentioned Biola University. Then a short time later his best friend also suggested Biola and offered to give him a ride to the university on his motorcycle. Perhaps God was trying to tell him something! Bob Vernon completed his undergraduate work at Biola.

He was drafted into the army. Not wanting to be in the infantry, he volunteered for the Air Force. He passed the physical and written tests, but a psychiatrist flunked him on the mental test because Bob professed he was a Christian. As a result, he was released from the military. Bob felt God was telling him he should not be a pilot.

When Bob returned home, he applied to be a policeman with the Los Angeles Police Department. His dad had been a policeman for twenty years with the LAPD. Bob passed the oral, written, physical and medical tests. There was just one more test to go. Again it was the psychiatric test.

The psychiatrist asked him about his spiritual life. He thought about not saying anything regarding Christianity, but instead professed that he believed in Christ. To his amazement, the psychiatrist said it was great for someone to know what he believes.

Bob rose in rank to become the Assistant Chief of Police of the Los Angeles Police Department, a position he held for ten years. He served under Chief Darryl Gates and had many experiences with high-profile crimes. As Assistant Chief he was in charge of all departmental operations for Los Angeles' eighteen police stations, supervising three thousand civilian workers and 7,800 officers. He retired after thirty-eight years of service. He also received a Masters in Business Administration from Pepperdine University and graduated from the University of Southern California's Managerial Policy Institute and the FBI's National Executive Institute.[3]

Because of his skill in management and his ability to foster a team spirit among the officers, he was often asked to speak to civic groups, schools, companies, etc. He has authored many books on leadership and always bases his presentations and books on biblical principles.

Since the late 1950s he has been involved with Hume Ministries, serving at one time as director of the high school camps. In 1994 he founded the Pointman Leadership Institute (PLI) under the Hume Ministries umbrella.[4] Leadership training by PLI is based on biblical principles and their highly-qualified instructors present character-based, ethical leadership seminars. They have reached attendees in fifty-two countries through 550 seminars involving forty thousand leaders.

Whenever Bob Vernon accepts an invitation to speak, he states up front that he will speak only if he can base what he is going to talk about on the foundation of biblical principles.

Bob is the author of many books and has traveled across the United States speaking of the need for change in the moral fiber of our nation. His message, based on the Christian ethic, is well received by both secular and religious groups.

One time he was asked to speak to a group of very influential millionaires in Chicago. He told them he would agree to speak, if he could share Christ. They agreed. There were two hundred fifty millionaires in the audience. After he spoke, fifty of them became Christians.

Truly, God answered his question about what he should do with his life.

Reaching the Unreachable

Dr. Alvin Low is president of ACTS International. Though he graduated at the top of his class in the Business Department of his college in Singapore, he chose not to take the path of a lucrative career in the business world.

He earned two Doctorates of Theology (Dallas Theological Seminary and Trinity Theological Seminary) and founded ACTS International. Additionally, he has more than thirty years of preaching and teaching experience in over forty countries and is the author of fourteen books. He is an adjunct professor at both the Dallas Seminary and the Denver Seminary.[1]

The mission/vision statement of ACTS is:

> "ACTS envisioned the establishment of training institutes in every country of Asia by the year 2020 in order to equip national pastoral leaders for effective ministry and church planting in every people group of Asia.[2]

The ACTS website may be found at: www.actsinternational.net.

Like Evantell and Operation Mobilisation, ACTS realizes that the training of local national pastors and church planters is more efficient than sending foreign missionaries. The native trainees already know the local language and culture. They are able to access unreached peoples and villages that are inaccessible to foreign missionaries. Estimates show that the cost to support ONE foreign missionary per year is around $80,000. This same amount will train more than fifty native pastors and church planters per year! It is also estimated that only 0.001% of Christian giving is targeted toward reaching the unreached (those who have not heard the Gospel of Jesus).

Asia has more than 55% of the world's population, and the most unreached peoples in the world.

The chart below was taken from the ACTS website:[3]

Country	Peoples	# Unreached Peoples
India	2332	2082
China	499	406
Pakistan	401	386
Bangladesh	370	336
Nepal	315	292

In the world today there are approximately 6.7 billion people. It is estimated that 1.6 billion of them have never heard of Jesus Christ and are considered to be unreached peoples. Of the 6.7 billion people, 1.8 billion are Christians and 3.3 billion more have access to the Gospel, but are not Christians.

This means that nearly 25% of the people in the world have never heard of Jesus. And, nearly 50% of those who have heard of Him have not yet become Christians. China has 1.4 billion people. Approximately one hundred million of them are believers (only God knows exactly how many for sure.) Though that number seems large, it is really a small percentage of the entire population of that country.

God is making the training of local servants of God possible for the ACTS organization. He has His own timing for opening the door to those areas which are very dangerous and may even be under siege, areas which could expose the trainees to persecution and war. The people of ACTS are careful to wait on Him. While they wait, they pray and prepare by translating their training material into the local languages of the peoples of Asia.

The unreached may never hear the Gospel in their lifetime. Many do not have any hope of hearing a Christian witness, unless a missionary from their own country is able to reach them where they live. Some of the churches that have been planted are made up of only a handful of believers. Other churches may have as many as several dozen believers. The Word of God is often preached from house to house with permission granted by the chiefs of the village. Bible studies are frequently held at night. Overall, efforts are in place for millions to hear the Good News of the Gospel and that Jesus is going to come again. The timing is in God's hands.

GOD'S WORD CANNOT BE FROZEN

North of the Arctic Circle in Russian Siberia's Yamal peninsula is a missionary who shares the Gospel with nomadic tribes and tells them about the love of Jesus Christ. The Yamal peninsula juts out nearly 435 miles into the Kara Sea. It is the site of one of the world's largest gas and oil discoveries. The word Yamal means "the end of the world", and the area fits its name.

Peter Khudi is one of a handful of Christian missionaries in that area. He is a member of a tribe called the Nenets, who are nomadic reindeer herders. It is the largest of the nomadic tribes, and Peter Khudi has been taking the Gospel to them and other tribes of that area for a number of years. He says, "When I became a Christian, God gave me a new heart. He also gave me new heart for my people."[1]

In Yamal, people depend on the reindeer for nearly everything—food, transportation, clothes, shoes, their tepee type homes, etc. Summer and winter the temperatures there range between -30 and -60 degrees Fahrenheit. In the winter the sun shines for only a few hours, but when it rises around noon, it is a spectacular sight.

When Peter Khudi first began his missionary work, he used reindeer for transportation. Today he uses a snowmobile as his main means of getting around, allowing him to travel further to evangelize to other families. Like some areas in Alaska, frozen rivers and lakes provide the highways for the snowmobiles. Cell phones permit him to keep in touch with the people, and generators make life a little easier.

Peter estimates that more than 500 Nenets people have accepted Christ as their Savior in recent years. Thank God for people like Peter Khudi who are willing to endure the harshness of Siberia to carry out the great commission of Jesus Christ. *"Go therefore and make disciples of all the nations, baptizing them in the name of the Father and the Son and the Holy Spirit, teaching them to observe all that I commanded you; and lo, I am with you always, even to the end of the age"* (Mathew 28:19-20).

TRAGEDY LEADS TO LIFE MISSION

In 1967, at the age of 17, Joni Eareckson Tada suffered a diving accident that resulted in a broken neck.[1] She was hospitalized and paralyzed as a quadriplegic. During two years of rehabilitation, she struggled with anger, depression and thoughts of suicide, unable to understand why God had let this happen to her. Rehab taught her how to live with her disabilities.

While in rehab she immersed herself in God's Word and emerged from it with renewed spiritual strength and the desire to help others in similar situations. She even learned how to paint with a brush held between her teeth. She became so proficient, that she was able to sell her artwork.

Joni has written many books, including her autobiography, *Joni*, which became an international best-seller and was distributed in many languages. She starred in a feature film made in 1979 based on the book. It told of her accident, struggles and life after rehab.

Her story is truly an inspiration for others, as she has devoted her life to a ministry of serving other people with disabilities. In 1979 she founded Joni and Friends (JAF), a Christian ministry for the disabled throughout the world. The growth of the organization made possible the establishment of the Joni and Friends International Disability Center (IDC) in 2006. Her work expresses her strong belief and trust in the Lord, expressed by the Bible verse, *"And we know that God causes all things to work together for good to those who love God, to those who are called according to His purpose"* (Romans 8:28).

Joni and her husband, Ken Tada, married in 1982. Ken was a teacher for thirty-two years. He joined Joni at the foundation in

2004. They both serve as permanent members of the International Board of Directors of Joni and Friends.

The Joni and Friends International Disability Center has created several flagship programs. They include a daily five-minute radio program that is broadcast over one thousand outlets. In 2002 it was awarded the "Radio Program of the Year" award by the National Religious Broadcasters. The Center also offers family retreats and supports a program called Wheels for the World. Wheelchairs are collected and refurbished by prison inmates and then donated to disabled children or adults in developing nations, along with a presentation of the Gospel. Physical therapists make sure each chair fits the disabled person it is given to.

Joni was appointed to the Disability Advisory Committee of the U. S. State Department in 2005. She travels extensively as a conference speaker and has written many articles for Christian publications, like *Christianity Today* and *Today's Christian Woman*.

In November 2009 Joni signed the Manhattan Declaration.[2] It is an ecumenical statement that calls on evangelicals, Catholics and orthodox Christians not to comply with rules and laws that permit abortion, same-sex marriage and other matters that go against one's own religious conscience.

In June 2010 Joni announced that she had been diagnosed with malignant breast cancer (Stage 3).[3] She met this challenge with the same unfaltering faith she has had all the years she has been disabled.

During an appearance on the Larry King Show she said, "We don't need to hold quadriplegia, pain, cancer or any other suffering in contempt—it just may be the open door to joy and peace for those who are paralyzed by unbelief (in Jesus) and blind to deeper, more satisfying truths (of God)."⁴ She underwent surgery for the cancer. Since the surgery and chemo treatments, the cancer has gone into remission. Joni has returned to her work and travels.

Named as the 2011 Honorary Chairman of the National Day of Prayer Task Force, Joni was quoted as saying, "I'm so grateful to God He has given me the health and stamina to call the people of our nation into faithful and specific prayer for our country. I look forward to fulfilling my responsibilities in this important role and I trust the Lord will use me to inspire and encourage others to cultivate a lifetime habit of prayer!"⁵ Further information on her work and organization may be found at: www.joniandfriends.org/.

Quote by Joni Eareckson: "Sometimes God allows what he hates to accomplish what He loves."⁶

TELL IT THROUGH EVANGELISM

"For nearly 40 years EvanTell has existed for one purpose . . . to declare the Gospel clearly and simply around the world, and equip believers to do the same through resources, events, training, and mentoring."[1]

Their stated mission is:
> "Declare the Gospel, Clearly and Simply
> Activate Believers Around the World
> Prepare Upcoming Generations to Reach the Lost"[2]

Evangelist and author Dr. Larry Moyer is the founder of EvanTell. He has empowered more than 200,000 believers across six continents to share the Gospel in a simple manner that has produced more than 13 million presentations of the Gospel.[3] This is done through evangelistic events and training seminars.

He has a simple way of sharing the Gospel through the "May I Ask You a Question" method distributed in tract form. His seminars called, "You Can Tell It!" and "You Can Preach It", teach how to share the Gospel in a way that can be used anytime, anywhere, and to anyone.[4]

EvanTell uses the method of helping other ministry organizations and churches to train their members to share the Gospel and evangelize the unsaved in their own areas and cultures. This approach has proved to be financially less expensive and less time-consuming than trying to send people to each country where they would first need to learn the local language and culture before hoping to spread the Word. Training local people means they can start right away. They have already developed relationships and often can take the Gospel into areas where missionaries are forbidden to go.

Another one of EvanTell's projects is to train staff members in pregnancy centers to provide them with faith-based, life-affirming instruction. The program is called *Save the Mother, Save Her Child.*[5] The goal is to train and equip every staff member and volunteer in pregnancy resource centers (PRC) across the United States. These staff members can then share the Gospel clearly and simply with each crisis pregnancy patient. This program is provided at no cost to the centers. It has proved to be most effective.

Further details are available at the website: www.savethemothersaveherchild.org/.

Dr. Larry Moyer has written many books and articles dealing with evangelism. His books include:

> *31 Days to Walking with God in the Workplace,*
> *Free and Clear,*
> *Show Me How to Share the Gospel,*
> *31 Days with the Master Fisherman,*
> *31 Days to Living as a New Believer,* and
> *21 Things God Never Said*

In addition to many speaking engagements around the United States, Dr. Moyer serves as visiting professor at Dallas Theological Seminary and is a guest lecturer at Word of Life Bible Institute.[6]

Besides its influence in the United States, EvanTell reaches the lost in a number of areas in Asia, Africa, Europe, South America and other parts of the world. Their very ambitious goal is to initiate training to 250 million people to show them how to present the gospel clearly and simply. That's ten percent of believers worldwide![7]

Further information is available on their web site: www.evantell.org/.

The Gospel Declared Through Sports

Sports play an important role in today's world. Sports celebrities are created when players are exceptionally successful in their sport. They always have a huge following of avid fans. Some fans enjoy watching or attending every game or event. Others are into statistics or the collecting of memorabilia. Still others enjoy talking about a sports win or loss with friends and family. There is a great feeling of loyalty to a certain sports figure or team by the fans, and most often it is a very exhilarating and fun experience. The celebrity player becomes a hero and is looked up to by young and old alike.

Sports figure celebrities may present a positive or negative influence on the fans. It all depends on how they display teamwork and sportsmanship, as well as the way they live their lives outside the public arena. Avid fans tend to emulate their heroes' actions, attitudes and viewpoints. When these are positive and provide good role models, they have a very beneficial effect.

There are many Christian athletes who are good role models. They take their star status seriously and know that how they live and play can influence the behavior and attitude of their fans. The following stories are about some athletes who are very aware of this responsibility to their fans. They use their public platform as an opportunity to witness about their Christian beliefs. They have no hesitation talking about the importance of God in their lives and know that their athletic ability is a gift from the Lord. Perhaps the Lord sees such special persons as part of His plan to spread the Word.

Here are a few stories about some of these super athletes and their testimonies.

USING HIS SECOND CHANCE

Josh Hamilton was born to be a baseball player. When he was just six years old, he was already playing quality ball on an 11-12 year-old team. He practiced constantly and worked hard to become an excellent ball player. Josh was drafted when he was just eighteen years old. This was in 1999, when the Tampa Bay Marlins chose him in the first round of the draft that year.[1]

When he was selected, the Tampa Bay team gave him a four million dollar bonus to sign with them. He joined their minor league system. At the start of his professional career Hamilton's parents even quit their jobs so they could travel with their son. He was really in the money and things were going well—until a spiral of bad decisions, drugs and alcohol took over his life and all went downhill.

Just before the start of the 2001 season, Hamilton and his parents were in a car wreck. His parents recuperated from their injuries, but Josh suffered a back injury that kept him from playing at his peak, and he sank into depression. He spent long hours at a tattoo shop, where he had multiple tattoos marked on his body. He was introduced to alcohol and drugs that developed into a strong cocaine addiction.

Due to his injury and the drug and alcohol addictions, Josh played only sporadically the next few years. He was introduced to crack and spent just about all of his money, including his signing bonus, to support his habit. He was completely out of baseball for the 2004 through 2006 seasons. He tried rehabilitation several times, but all efforts along that line failed—until he met Jesus Christ.

In his book, *Beyond Belief: Finding the Strength to Come Back*,[2] written with Tim Keown, Josh makes no excuses. He accepts the blame for all the poor decisions he made. His book tells his story about his battle with the demons he faced and overcame. When giving a brief summary of his recovery, Hamilton simply says, "It's a God thing." He adds, "I have been given a platform to tell my story. I pray every night I am a good messenger".[3]

Josh witnesses openly to groups and fans telling them how Jesus brought him back from the brink and how his faith keeps him in line. His father-in-law, Michael Chadwick, said, "The odds of getting off of crack are about one percent and the odds of going back to a baseball field don't exist. Somebody forgot to tell God."[4]

In 2008 Hamilton joined the Texas Rangers and started for them in the outfield. In the All Star game home run derby that summer, Josh Hamilton set a new record with twenty-eight homers in the first round.[5] In 2010 Josh was voted the American League's MVP (most valuable player).[6] He proved to be a key player in leading the Rangers to two consecutive World Series in 2010 and 2011.

The Rangers have given Josh team-wide support. In a special tribute to him by his teammates, their division wins were celebrated with ginger ale, rather than champagne so Josh could participate in the celebration. Josh is an admitted alcoholic.

Josh Hamilton has committed to memory and relies on this Bible verse: *"Submit therefore to God. Resist the devil and he will flee from you"* (James 4:7).[7]

Josh has had relapses in his daily battle with his addictions. He admits he is a "sinful man" and has moments of "weakness".[8] He is very open about his failings, and willingly faces the media and his fans. He has made public apologies when he has had a back-slide and always reaffirms his Christian faith.

Because of the adversity Josh Hamilton has faced, the outstanding skills that God has given him, and the renewal he has realized through Christ in his life, Josh has the platform to witness to others about Jesus and His grace.

Miracles, Prophecy and God's Other Ways

AN MVP FOR CHRIST

Emmitt Smith was a phenomenal football player. Born in Pensacola, Florida, on May 15, 1969, Emmitt Smith knew by the time he was six years old that he wanted to play professional football.

At his induction into the Football Hall of Fame in Canton, Ohio, on August 8, 2010, he began his speech with: "Thank you to my Lord and Savior Jesus Christ for blessing me to play the sport I so dearly love for almost three decades."[1]

He continued with this story. "When I was six years old, I was watching the Dallas Cowboys on television with my father and some of our relatives. I clearly remember turning to my father and saying, 'One day I'm going to play professional football, and I'm going to play for the Dallas Cowboys.'"[2] His father agreed that would be a good goal for him to have. This gave Emmitt tremendous support. From then on he worked with great passion and dedication to realize his dream. He didn't even care what position he played, as long as he was out there playing!

Emmitt excelled at football in high school and in 1986 was named player of the year by both *USA Today* and *Parade Magazine*. He went on to The University of Florida on an athletic scholarship and starred with the Florida Gators. He set fifty-eight school records in the three years he was there, 1987-1989. Some of these records remain unbroken to this day. He also earned All-American honors.[3]

In 1990 Emmitt Smith was projected to be one of the top ten players to be drafted into the National Football League. He was about to do something he had always dreamed about: play professional football. That year the Dallas Cowboys did not have a pick in the top ten players. They traded up to get Emmitt as the seventh selection in the overall draft.

The phone rang and he got THE call from the head coach of the Dallas Cowboys, Jimmy Johnson, asking him if he would like to wear the star of the Dallas Cowboys. Emmitt could hardly believe this was happening to him. It was God's confirmation that his childhood dream was part of God's direction for his life. Had he been chosen in the top ten, he very likely would have been drafted by Tampa Bay or Seattle instead of the Dallas Cowboys.

Emmitt Smith became the NFL's all-time rushing leader. He played on three Super Bowl winning Dallas Cowboys teams. He is the only running back to ever win a Super Bowl championship, the NFL Most Valuable Player award, the NFL rushing award, and the Super Bowl Most Valuable Player award, all in the same season 1993. Emmitt retired as a Dallas Cowboy in 2005.

From his youth, his parents had always preached to Emmitt the importance of education and that it was something that would last him a lifetime. He promised his mother he would complete his college degree. During the off season, when he wasn't playing football for the Dallas Cowboys, he returned to classes at the University of Florida. He kept his promise to his mother when he earned his degree in Public Recreation in May, 1996.

Emmitt Smith is a devout Christian and family man. He and his wife, Patricia, have a son, Emmitt IV, and daughters Rheagen, Jasmin and Skylar.

His excellence in football has given him a platform to tell the world about Jesus.

As it says in Psalm 139:14, "*I will give thanks to You, for I am fearfully and wonderfully made.*"

THE PHOENIX OF NEW ORLEANS

Drew Brees was born in Dallas in 1979 and grew up in Austin, Texas. Playing sports was an integral part of his family's life. Drew went to Westlake High School, where he earned letters in football, basketball and baseball. As the school's quarterback his senior year in 1996, he led his team to a 16-0 record and the 5A State Championship. He earned the 5A Offensive Player of the Year that year as well.[1]

Drew did not look like a regular quarterback, as he stood almost six foot tall and was very thin. But he knew the game and had a throwing arm that threw the ball with accuracy and force. All of this was accomplished though he had suffered a possible career-ending knee injury the end of his junior year.

One Sunday in the summer before that fantastic senior year, Drew was in church with his family. He heard something that day that changed his life. He had walked into church on crutches because of the torn ACL. He was seventeen years old and the thought crossed his mind about what he would do if he didn't have football or some other sport in his life. He wondered what that would mean for the rest of his life.

The minister made an appeal to the congregation that morning. He said that God was looking for a few good men to work for Him and represent the Christian faith. Drew remembers thinking to himself that he would like to be one of those men.

Drew became a Christian that day. He had new resolve to let nothing stand in his way.

He finished his senior year with a 28-0 high school career record. He earned a scholarship to Purdue University, where he led the Boilermakers to the Rose Bowl in 2001. Drew was a two-time Heisman finalist, lettered all four years of his college career, and won other collegiate awards. In addition, he earned a degree in Industrial Management from the Krannert School of Management at Purdue.[2]

After graduation Drew Brees was drafted by the San Diego Chargers, where he spent five seasons. At the end of the last season, he dislocated his throwing shoulder while trying to recover a fumble. This put his career in jeopardy again. He was given a twenty-five percent chance of being able to heal and return to playing. He could have easily given up with doubt and resignation. Instead, he remembered his commitment that day in church when he was in high school. He knew God had a plan for him. He just had to rely on that and believe God would see him through this stumbling block.

Drew fully recovered from the injury in two months. He then had to make a choice to move on to a new team, and he chose the New Orleans Saints. It was a losing team located in a city still reeling from the tragedy of Hurricane Katrina. He and his wife decided that they would be "part of something much greater than just being part of a team—they would be part of rebuilding a city."[3] That was in 2006, and four seasons later the New Orleans Saints were victors in the Super Bowl!

Drew Brees and his wife Brittany continue to give hope to New Orleans and the state of Louisiana through the creation of the Brees Dream Foundation. The foundation has committed over six million dollars to advance cancer research. It provides care for cancer patients and has helped restore what was lost in the hurricane damage. They have rebuilt schools, parks, playgrounds and athletic fields, not only in Louisiana, but also in San Diego and West Lafayette, Indiana.

Drew Brees has written a book, *Coming Back Stronger—Unleashing the Hidden Power of Adversity.* In it he tells of his journey, and emphasizes why he never gives up because he knows he is following God's plan for his life.

Drew Brees has a platform to talk about his faith. He says, "I live for God, for the faith that I have in Him. Knowing the sacrifices that Jesus Christ made on the cross for me and feeling like it's in God's hands, all I have to do is just give my best, commit the rest to Him."[4] Drew knows God will take care of everything else.

Par Excellence for Christ

The Fellowship of Christian Athletes (FCA) was started in 1954 and has become the largest Christian sports organization in the United States.[1] FCA works with coaches and athletes in the professional arena, as well as coaches and athletes in colleges, high schools, junior highs and with youth.

The vision of FCA is "to see the world impacted for Jesus Christ through the influence of athletes and coaches." Their mission is "to present to athletes and coaches and all whom they influence the challenge and adventure of receiving Jesus Christ as Savior and Lord, serving Him in their relationships and in the fellowship of the church."[2] The organization stresses the importance by members of a true commitment to Jesus and His Word by honoring the values of integrity, service, teamwork and excellence.

FCA is represented in many sports, one of which is golf. In the United States there are over one hundred million golfers and fans. Close to five million of these are youth.[3] FCA Junior Golf Camps provide excellent golf instruction in beautiful settings, along with outstanding sports training, inspiring speakers and loads of fun. These camps give FCA an opportunity to spread the Gospel and provide leadership training.

Zach Johnson is one of the professional golfers who has teamed up with FCA. He gladly speaks about his faith. He openly encourages other athletes and coaches to commit and deepen their lives in Christ. Golfers may recognize him as the 2007 winner of the Masters Tournament in Augusta, Georgia. After winning he talked about his Christian faith and thanked God saying, "This being Easter (April 8, 2007), I cannot help but believe my Lord and Savior, Jesus Christ was walking with me. I owe this (win) to Him."[4]

Zack Johnson has also won the AT&T Classic (2007), the Sony Open in Hawaii (2009), along with more than twenty other professional golf tournaments. He was born in Iowa and raised in Cedar Rapids. After the extensive flooding in Cedar Rapids in 2008, he organized the PGA Tour Flood Relief effort through a one-day golf event held in the city.

The Zach Johnson Foundation was started in July of 2010 and was formed to benefit children in need in the greater Cedar Rapids area. The largest fund raiser for the Foundation is an annual golf tournament, called the Zach Johnson Foundation Classic, co-sponsored by AEGON/Transamerica. It is held at the Elmcrest Country Club in Cedar Rapids, where Johnson got his start.

The inaugural tournament was held on August 1, 2011, and raised nearly a half-million dollars for the educational program called *Kids on Course.* Zach Johnson and his wife generously matched the money raised.[5] Many local and national sports figures attended the event, along with several thousand spectators. The funds raised are used to help make it possible for Cedar Rapids elementary school children to realize their academic potential.

Johnson has said, "It is very easy for me and my wife to be associated with organizations like FCA that really have a heart for Jesus. Because sports are so ingrained in our culture, that is a great platform, and it's great to both share from it and be a part of it."[6]

Jim Esary, national director of the FCA Golf ministry, says that golf is a game of rules and proper behavior. All players have to think about how they act and perform on the course. He notes that the players who are Christians take being a gentlemen a step further, as they also use opportunities to witness about their faith.

They are willing to help on and off the course when they can, using their celebrity status to help further the name of Jesus. He considers Zach to be one of those guys. Zach is never hesitant to show what it means to be a follower of Christ.

For further information, refer to the website: www.zachjohnsonfoundation.com.

Witnessing With His Eyes

After an astonishing college career as the star quarterback for the University of Florida, Tim Tebow was a first-round pick by the Denver Broncos in 2010. He had earned many unparalleled honors and awards, among them two national championships. He was the first sophomore in NCAA history to win the Heisman Trophy.[1]

In his book *Through My Eyes*, he tells the story of his strong Christian faith, his life and his career.

Tim was born in 1987 in the Philippines to Christian missionaries Bob and Pam Tebow. During the pregnancy, his mother suffered a life-threatening infection that required strong drugs to wake her from a coma and to treat severe dysentery. Doctors predicted that the baby would be stillborn and advised that an abortion would be the only answer to save her life. However, Pam Tebow discarded any thought of abortion. She carried the baby to full term and delivered a healthy child.

After returning to the United States, the Tebows lived in Jacksonville, Florida, where Tim and his siblings were home-schooled. This instilled in Tim a strong Christian belief, which he professes today. He continues to excel as an outstanding athlete, never losing his devotion to his beliefs.

There are times Tim's strong position as a devout Christian have made him a provocative figure. As a Florida Gator quarterback he printed the Bible reference Philippians 4:13 on his eye black (adhesive sticker that provides anti-glare protection):

"I can do all things through Him who strengthens me." He used this verse every game throughout his collegiate career. It is impossible to know how many people saw this verse and referred to it.

How God Works in Today's World

Tim continued using this verse until one very crucial game, when he felt the need to change the eye-black reference to John 3:16, *"For God so loved the world, that He gave His only begotten Son, that whoever believes in Him shall not perish, but have eternal life."*

Ninety-four million people accessed John 3:16 on Google during that game. Tim was overwhelmed by that and said, "Wow, how are 94 million people not knowing John 3:16? It's really awesome to see how God works in a very unique way when you just trust Him and put a little Bible verse under your eyes."[2]

One of the thirty-second commercials aired during Super Bowl XLIV (2010) supported the pro-life view he shares with *Focus on the Family*. Though the word abortion was never mentioned, both Tim and his mother appeared in the ad and depicted the strong pro-life position that they have taken and the strong Christian belief they share.

Tim Tebow became the #1 quarterback for the Denver Broncos. Since both the NCAA and the NFL banned any writing on a player's eye black in 2010, Tim is no longer able to display a Scripture message.

There is another way that Tim honors the Lord. After something good happens during a game, he bends down on one knee to pray and thank the Lord. Many now call it "Tebowing". With this action Tim shows his humility before the Lord as he gives thanks. It is his way to express his feelings about the only thing that matters to him more than football.

Just think, if Tim's mother had taken the doctor's advice and aborted her baby, we wouldn't be reading about Tim Tebow today.

In a playoff game in 2012 between the Pittsburgh Steelers and the Denver Broncos, Tim Tebow passed for 316 yards and averaged 31.6 yards per pass. The TV rating for that game was 31.6! Was this one of God's OTHER WAYS to remind us of John 3:16?

THE GOSPEL EXPRESSED THROUGH MUSIC

From the book of Genesis to the book of Revelation there are hundreds of references to music, singing, songs and dancing in the Bible.

As defined in the dictionary, the word psalm means: "A sacred song or hymn, in particular any of those contained in the biblical Book of Psalms and used in Christian and Jewish worship."[1]

Since music plays an important role in God's Word, it should be no surprise that in today's world He also uses music to work His will.

The following stories illustrate some of the ways music is used to spread His Word.

Miracles, Prophecy and God's Other Ways

Faith Survives Life's Tragedies

Horatio Spafford was inspired to write the hymn *It Is Well With My Soul* as his heart ached with loss and despair. The depth of his sorrow is expressed in the hymn, but it also affirms his faith in God's goodness, love, power and provision. The hymn has meant much to those who need reassurance during trouble they are experiencing. It is another way God makes Himself known in today's world.

This hymn was written after several traumatic events in Spafford's life. He and his wife, Anna, had five children, four girls and a son, Horatio, Jr. The family lived a charmed life in Chicago in the late 1860s. He was a successful lawyer and very active in reform movements and supported evangelical leaders like Dwight L. Moody. He was a dedicated Christian and served as a church elder in the Presbyterian Church. Spafford was a very wealthy man through wise investments made in real estate located on the shores of Lake Michigan. Then tragedy struck.

The first blow was the death in 1870 of his only son at age four from scarlet fever. Then came the Great Chicago Fire in 1871, which destroyed most of Stafford's holdings. The Spafford home was not burned, and his family was safe, but they were in financial ruin. Even then they used what resources they had to help others who were homeless, hungry, sick and in even worse despair.

Anna's health was not good, and in 1873 Spafford decided to take a trip to Europe to put the tragedies behind them. Spafford planned not only to visit Europe, but he was also invited to assist Dwight L. Moody and Ira D. Sankey in a revival they were leading in England.

The Spaffords booked passage on the Ville du Havre for a departure in November, 1873. At the last minute, Spafford had a business emergency and could not accompany his family and sent them on without him. He planned to join them later. During the voyage the Ville du Havre was struck by a British iron sailing ship in the middle of the Atlantic. The ship sank within twelve minutes. Only 81 of the 307 crew and passengers survived. Though Anna Spafford was spared, all four of the Spafford daughters drowned. Anna was taken to Cardiff, Wales, and her telegram to her husband said: "Saved alone. What shall I do . . ."[1]

Horatio immediately booked passage to bring his wife home. During the voyage the captain called him to the bridge and said to Horatio, "A careful reckoning has been made and I believe we are now passing the place where the Ville du Havre was wrecked. The water is three miles deep."[2]

That night when he was alone in his cabin, Horatio G. Spafford wrote the words to the famous hymn, *It Is Well With My Soul*. Despite his grief and the tragedies, his faith in God had not faltered.

Horatio and his wife came back to Chicago to try to build a new life. They were blessed with three more children, a son and two daughters. This son was also named Horatio, Jr. in honor of their lost son. Then tragedy struck them again, when little four year old Horatio died of scarlet fever just like the brother before him!

The Spaffords decided to leave America and move to Jerusalem, which they did with a few of their friends in 1881. They started a mission work called The American Colony, which served the poor and needy, cared for those who were ill, and took in homeless children. They just wanted to show the love of God to others. Horatio G. Spafford died of malaria in Jerusalem at age sixty, October 16, 1888.

As a postscript to the story, during and immediately after World War I, the American Colony played a critical role in supporting communities that surrounded Jerusalem. The group helped relieve the great sufferings and deprivations caused by the war and ran soup kitchens, hospitals, orphanages and other charitable ventures.

The words in Spafford's hymn were based on 2 Kings 4:26. Few could come through so many senseless tragedies and still maintain their faith in God, praising His goodness with no resentment and blame. The hymn has comforted many who are in despair, yet assures them that God will sustain them through it all.

It Is Well With My Soul

When peace like a river, attendeth my way,
When sorrows like sea billows roll;
Whatever my lot, Thou hast taught me to say,
It is well, it is well, with my soul.

Refrain:
It is well, with my soul, It is well, with my soul,
It is well, it is well, with my soul.

Though Satan should buffet, though trials should come,
Let this blest assurance control,
That Christ has regarded my helpless estate,
And hath shed His own blood for my soul.

My sin, oh the bliss of this glorious thought!
My sin not in part but the whole,
Is nailed to the cross, and I bear it no more,
Praise the Lord, praise the Lord, O my soul!

For me, be it Christ, be it Christ hence to live:
If Jordan above me shall roll,
No pang shall be mine, for in death as in life,
Thou wilt whisper Thy peace to my soul.

But, Lord, 'tis for Thee, for Thy coming we wait,
The sky, not the grave, is our goal;
Oh, trump of the angel! Oh, voice of the Lord!
Blessed hope, blessed rest of my soul.

And Lord, haste the day when my faith shall be sight,
The clouds be rolled back as a scroll:
The trump shall resound, and the Lord shall descend,
Even so, it is well with my soul.

The tune for the hymn was composed by Philip Bliss. Bliss called it *Ville du Havre*, named after the sunken vessel that took so many lives.

A Musician Since Childhood

Contemporary Christian musician, David Meese, has been a recording artist for more than thirty years. He grew up in Humble, Texas, and was considered a child prodigy on the piano. He had an abusive, alcoholic father, and his earliest happy memories mostly revolve around the piano. He remembers wanting so much to be able to play and press the keys. Because he was too small to get up on the piano bench by himself, someone had to help him. Once he was on the bench, he recalls being very happy.[1]

He began touring as a concert pianist at the age of ten. When he was fourteen, he performed the Mozart piano Concerto in F Major with the Houston Chamber Orchestra. At fifteen he won a nationwide talent show and as a result toured England, Germany, France, Switzerland and Holland. At sixteen he was the featured soloist with the Houston Symphony. Renowned conductor Andre Previn directed his performance of the difficult Khachaturian Piano Concert, which is forty-five minutes in length.

He received a full scholarship to the Peabody Conservatory of Music in Baltimore. This is where he made a serious commitment to follow Christ. There he met his future wife, Debbie. She was also a student, majoring in viola. David credits her with keeping things together during tough times. She is his stabilizing help-mate.

David and Debbie Meese have been married over thirty years. They have two children, who are also involved in music performance. Debbie has written a wonderful devotional to go along with David's signature CD, *Once in a Lifetime*. David continues to play for audiences around the world, from the huge auditoriums of famous concert halls to the smallest of churches. He has a humorous perspective and outlook that gives a memorable comic relief that still gets across his serious message. He feels God has called him to share his walk through personal despair and through his journey of forgiveness.

He often introduces his autobiographical song, *My Father's Chair*, by telling about one memory he has of his father, who would always sit in the same chair to watch television when he came home from work. Because he was an alcoholic with a violent temper, the abuse David experienced at his hand has erased other memories of his father. It was like his father disappeared.

In the first verse of the song, he talks about his father's chair, but it is empty. The second verse is about David's chair and how he hopes his children will see his chair as a place that is full of love and acceptance.

Then, in the third verse, David makes a wonderful discovery. He explains in the song that the Father in heaven is his real Father, whose chair is His heavenly throne. This Father is always with him, and someday all of His children will gather around His chair in heaven to live with Him forever.

David Meese has a clear message: Total surrender to God in trust and obedience.

"I'm convinced that there has been a tremendous urgency placed upon my life by the Holy Spirit, an urgency to get the Gospel out to as many people as possible," he said. "I believe God wants me to go and share the Gospel everywhere, anywhere people will have me. I've never felt this calling on my life so strongly, (as) I'm convinced Jesus is coming back very soon."[2]

Further information on David and his music ministry can be found on his website www.davidmeece.com.

Young Child, Big Voice for the Lord

She weighed only 4.1 lbs. at birth and spent the first three weeks of her life in ICU. Yet, by age nine she had already recorded three music albums, appeared on television world-wide and sung in a movie. She is an amazingly blessed and gifted Christian gospel singer.

Rhema Marvanne was born in September, 2002. Her mother died of cancer when she was just six years old. Her dad said she began singing about the time she began talking. When she was seven years old, Rhema made her first recording, singing *Amazing Grace*. She became an overnight singing sensation when her performance was put on the internet.

At age seven she was baptized. Today she is often called upon to sing in churches, for non-profit organizations, charities, hospitals and other special events.

Her first movie, called *Machine Gun Preacher* (a Lionsgate Film), *was* released in the fall of 2011. It is the story about a drug dealer who becomes a Christian and is baptized. During his baptism Rhema sings *Amazing Grace*. At that central point of the film he turns from being a bad guy into a good guy with a mission to help orphan children in Africa.

God in his mysterious way continues to further His kingdom by giving this young girl the incredible voice that has a world-wide ministry to those who hear her. She honors her mother as a Christian gospel singer and servant of the Lord. On her web site is this verse: *"For I know the plans I have for you, declares the Lord, plans for welfare and not for evil, to give you a future and a hope"* (Jeremiah 29:11).

Her music is available on iTunes and Amazon.com, as well as through her website on-line store at www.rhemamarvanne.com/.[1]

CHRISTIAN SONGWRITERS OF THE CENTURY

Gospel singers/songwriters Bill and Gloria Gaither are known to millions. Since the 1950s they have written or performed over seven hundred songs. Among these are well known gospel songs such as: *Because He Lives, He Touched Me, There's Something About That Name,* and *Let's Just Praise The Lord.*

Together they have won eight Grammy Awards and have been named the Gospel Music Association's "Songwriter of the Year" eight times.[1] In 2000 the American Society of Composer, Authors and Publishers (ASCAP) named them the Christian Songwriters of the Century![2]

At a concert with the Nashville Choir in May, 2011, host for the evening, Shelia Walsh, said that Bill and Gloria Gaither write songs with fruit on all the branches. "Some songs are like fruit on the lowest branch so that a child can reach (understand) them. Other songs meet the listener at eye level helping us to see life exactly where we are. Then there are songs that are on the highest branches of the tree—these songs help us to look up and long for heaven."[3]

Bill and Gloria Gaither are also wonderful mentors for other musical artists. Bill founded his first gospel quartet in 1956, The Bill Gaither Trio. He married Gloria in 1962, and they became a powerful duo in writing music and lyrics. Their full-time career was launched in 1967.

Though highly successful, they still maintain their lives in Bill's hometown in Alexandria, Indiana, in the same home they purchased as newlyweds. They have three grown children and five grandchildren. Throughout their career weekend-only tour performances have always been a top priority to maintain family time.

Next to the home is the Gaither Music compound, housing state-of-the-art studios. Their famous Homecoming videos, first made in 1991, are sometimes taped at these studios.

The Gaithers do not spend most of their profits on themselves. They have given $3 million to Anderson University and set up a $2.2 million Gospel Music Trust Fund to help aging musicians who have no retirement savings.

To the Gaithers, Christian music is about giving. Bill Gaither says "Our calling is not just making music . . . but communicating the reality of Christ. If we have done anything right over the years, I hope we have built bridges where people could connect with God and with each other."[4]

They surely have used their platform to spread the Word and proclaim the saving grace of our Savior.

The Gospel Advanced in the Business World

We live in a world where righteous living is often avoided and Christianity is frequently under attack. It is encouraging to realize that there are Christian companies in business, which make a profit, operate ethically and treat their employees well.

While there are many businesses run by Christians, there are only a few that state their Christian beliefs as part of the company's philosophy, mission and vision. They do not hesitate to state openly that their CEOs and founders are Christian believers. They proudly announce it on their websites and other marketing pieces, along with their mission and business philosophy statements. They follow Jesus' command to *"Let your light shine before men in such a way that they may see your good works, and glorify your Father who is in heaven"* (Mark 5:16).

As is true of music, business (buying, selling and trading) is often mentioned in both the Old and New Testaments of the Bible. Peter and Andrew were fishermen, the Apostle Paul was a tent maker, and Matthew was a tax collector. In the Old Testament, slaves were bought and sold; cattle, oxen and sheep were traded for money; land and crops were traded in return for money. So it is not surprising to find that God is using business as one of the ways He works in today's world.

Following you will find stories about some companies and the people who lead them.

CHICK-FIL-A

Chick-Fil-A was started in 1946, when S.Truett Cathy opened his first chicken outlet in Hapeville, Georgia. It was called the Dwarf Grill, so named because it had a dwarf-sized front door that children could enter through.

Now his world famous chicken sandwiches are sold in more than sixteen hundred Chick-Fil-A restaurants in thirty-nine states and Washington, D.C., making it the second largest fast food chicken chain in the country. In 2010 the company's annual sales were over $3.5 billion, representing an 11.37% increase over the company's 2009 performance.[1] Expansion plans call for growth in the Midwest and southern California.

2012 marks the sixty-seventh year that ninety-year-old S. Truett Cathy has been in the restaurant business. He currently serves as chairman of the company. He is a devout Christian who has taught Sunday school for over fifty-one years. His religious beliefs permeate the company to this day.

The corporate purpose statement shows the heart of the company and says that the business exists "To glorify God by being a faithful steward of all that is entrusted to us. To have a positive influence on all who come in contact with Chick-fil-A."[2]

Cathy has always emphasized the importance of responsibility and integrity in the workplace and in the home. He considers cohesion in the family to be of upmost important and sponsors seminars geared toward the family.

The company also provides a scholarship program for employees and has a foundation that sponsors a boys and girls camp. The WinShape Center Foundation has built fourteen foster homes in Georgia, Tennessee, Alabama and Brazil. The WinShape

Family Centre provides the setting for marital conferences and retreats for entire families. The company has provided a Bible for every school located in the state of Georgia.[3]

Chick-Fil-A is closed on Sundays, Thanksgiving and Christmas. Cathy says, "Our decision to close on Sunday was our way of honoring God and directing our attention to things more important than our business. If it took seven days to make a living with a restaurant, then we needed to be in some other line of work. Through the years I have never wavered from that position."[4]

HOBBY LOBBY

David Green founded Hobby Lobby in 1972, with a six hundred dollar loan and a three-hundred square-foot retail space.[1] Hobby Lobby now has over 490 stores in forty-one states. The average store size is 60,000 square feet.

The stores are open Monday through Saturday, excluding holidays. Hobby Lobby closes its stores by 8:00 p.m., and is the only billion-dollar company that does. All stores are closed on Sundays to allow time for employee families to worship. Green has said there could be more than $100 million in sales generated by being open nation-wide on Sundays, but he is firm about his priorities.

Christian music is played in all of the stores for the encouragement of staff and customers. David Green pays his employees several dollars above the minimum wage, and strives to maintain a deep loyalty to his employees as well as to the customers.

As he stated in an interview with ChristiaNet, "All the things we do, all our behavior, should let others know that we are living by, and operating in, Biblical principles. Principle and character are the highest quality traits on our list.[2]" He continued, "Our organization wants to be remembered as one that knows the difference between temporal and eternal."[3]

Green and his family have given millions to Christian causes and education. Their donations have benefited Liberty University and Oral Roberts University, and are helping to establish C.S. Lewis College in Massachusetts.[4] David Green and Hobby Lobby have provided over 200 million copies of the Gospels and have projects in place to distribute information about salvation to over 12.9 million homes.

Recently the company and Green have been involved with the project of purchasing Christian artifacts, biblical papyri, Hebrew scrolls, medieval manuscripts, rare Bibles and other sacred documents with the hope of creating a National Bible Museum. A proposed site for the museum is Dallas, Texas.[5]

David Green has a set the bar for successfully running a business and living his life according to Biblical principles.

Mardel Christian Stores

Mart Green is the son of David Green, the founder of Hobby Lobby. Mart started the Mardel chain of Christian stores when he was only nineteen years old. He opened its first location in Oklahoma City, Oklahoma, on June 1, 1981. Mardel has grown and currently has thirty-five retail operations, located in seven states.[1] It is part of the Hobby Lobby group of companies, though the two businesses are not affiliated.

In January, 2005, Mart Green was named by *Christian Retailing* as one of the Top Fifty People who have most impacted and shaped Christian retailing in the last half century. The 2008 Jim Carlson Christian Bookstore of the Year Award was presented to Mardel by CBS in July of that year.[2]

The mission statement for Mardel says: "Our mission is to equip the whole person by being a resource center that provides for spiritual and intellectual needs. *'For the equipping of the saints for the work of service, to the building up of the body of Christ; until we all attain to the unity of the faith, and of the knowledge of the Son of God'*[3] (Ephesians 4:12)."

The company donates ten percent of pre-tax profits to support their goal of providing Bibles around the world. Much of this donation is given to Wycliffe Bible Translators to facilitate the printing of Bibles in languages that have been translated by Wycliffe.[4]

The company slogan is "Renewing Minds—Transforming Lives", reflecting their vision to help change lives with the products they sell.

In November 2007 Mart Green pledged $70 million to Oral Roberts University (ORU), which went towards retiring much of the university's debt. An additional gift of $10 million was given to ORU in January, 2009, for campus renovations. In December, 2010, the Green family announced they would make a gift of another $10 million in 2011 to be used for renovations and technology improvements. This brings the total donations to ORU by the Greens to $110 million. Mart Green has served as Chairman of the Board at ORU since January 2008.[5]

Green is also founder and CEO of Bearing Fruit Communications, which produced the documentary *Beyond the Gates of Splendor.* His feature film production company, Every Tribe Entertainment, released the movie *End of the Spear* in 2006. The movie portrays the story of missionaries Jim and Elisabeth Elliot. The movie has had great impact and is now shown around the world.

INTERSTATE BATTERY SYSTEM OF AMERICA

Norm Miller is Chairman of the Board for Interstate Battery. He is also a believer in God's power to change lives, because he has experienced that.[1]

Norm started out as a salesman for Interstate Battery. He had a bad drinking habit, and drank as hard as he worked. He remembers how for twenty years he got drunk at least once a week, often drinking so heavily that he would black out. One night in 1974 he was driving home after drinking and was pulled over by a policeman.

This had happened before, as he already had two DWIs. Somehow he talked his way out of this one. When he woke up the next morning he had a terrible hangover and called in sick to work. It was that morning that the realization hit him—he was an alcoholic like his father had been. He was losing control of his life.

In desperation he blurted out, "God, help me! I can't handle it!" The Lord answered his plea and removed his desire to drink completely. Norm Miller realizes that it doesn't happen quickly and completely for everyone, but he is eternally thankful that it did for him. Before that morning he wouldn't have been able to tell you if he believed in God, because he had never thought about it. Religion meant nothing to him, and he never attended church.

A friend tried to share with Norm about the Bible and what it had to say. Norm just cut him off and told him that unless he could be convinced the Bible was the TRUTH, he couldn't accept it as anything but just another old book. His friend took the challenge and provided Norm with books and information that provided conclusive proof of the validity of the Bible and Jesus Christ as Savior. The books contained articles that described archaeological discoveries that proved facts in the Bible, as well as articles that told of historical discoveries which verified the authenticity of ancient Bible manuscripts.

Norm was especially impressed with the fulfillment of the Old Testament prophecy in the New Testament. He began reading the Bible and started attending a Bible study. Norm Miller finally accepted the Lord realizing he was described in the verse *"for all have sinned and fall short of the glory of God"* (Romans 3:23). He realized the Good News is that *"you will know the truth, and the truth will make you free"* (John 8:32).

Today Norm Miller thanks God for giving him the power to change his ruined life. It also changed the way he operated and treated people in the business world. He has made Christian business principles part of Interstate Batteries' corporate culture. Interstate maintains a full-time chaplain, and Norm Miller practices Christian values and evangelizes to others so they, too, can be *free*. He is also a Board Member of Dallas Theological Seminary.

This is the philosophy statement of Interstate Batteries:

"To treat others as we want to be treated; treating all our business associates with respect, fairness, and integrity; caring for and listening to them; professionally serving them; always being a model of working hard and striving toward excellence."[2]

JM Eagle Company

The JM Eagle Company is privately held, headed by Walter Wang, a born-again Christian. Walter grew up in a Christian home, as his grandfather had been converted by an American missionary who had come to Taiwan to spread the Word.

Walter's father was one of the world's richest men and founder of Formosa Plastics in Taiwan. His father purchased a plastic pipe division of another company, and Walter worked in Taiwan for a couple of years learning the business.

He bought the company from his father at a very fortunate time. Plastic piping was just catching on among cities which needed to replace older and decaying water systems. Walter moved the company to Los Angeles, where it continued its success. He seemed to be living a charmed life. His company grew to become the world's largest manufacturer of plastic pipe.[1]

Then, in 2006, tragedy struck. Wang was diagnosed with a rare form of nasal cancer at a stage four level. It had already spread to the base of the skull. He went to Hong Kong where hours of chemotherapy and radiation treatments began. Yet, true healing was realized only after heeding advice from a Christian friend. This led Wang to an encounter with the Holy Spirit.

Wang recalls the conversation he had with his friend, who had asked him if there was any unforgiveness in his life. The friend told him, "Jesus came to forgive each and every one of us. God's character is love, so therefore, He forgave."[2] He reminded Wang that Jesus even forgave those who crucified Him as He died for all of us on the cross.

He told Wang that he would never receive true healing until he stopped going against God's teachings and character and until he forgave all the persons he had problems with. Wang asked God to give him a heart of love to forgive and bless. He made a list of the people he needed to forgive.

He and his friend were in a small room as Wang prayed and forgave each person on his list, once and for all, in the name of Jesus. Suddenly, Wang felt warmth come into his body, starting from his head and going all the way down to his toes. He then began laughing hysterically. The laughter continued for more than ten minutes, and he was unable to control it. Then he had a feeling of a great burden being released from his heart, a burden that had been there a long time.

Wang was a changed man—he was born again. His wife, who was a Buddhist, became a Christian after she saw the dramatic transformation in her husband.

Five months later, after further treatment, Walter knew that God had healed him. He knew he had been put through the cancer burden to show him that the Lord is in control. Wang now feels that his position as head of the world's largest manufacturer of plastic pipe is a divine calling. He considers himself only acting CEO—the chair for the official position of chairman is empty. Walter trusts the Lord with everything in his life and in the company, as he lets God be the Chairman of the Board.

Wang feels he is in the position to contribute to society through his company. He can share his testimony, spread the Gospel and bring more people to Christ. In addition, he can physically change the world by bringing water, which he considers the "essence of life"[3], to peoples where clean water has never been experienced.

The JM Eagle Company has donated miles and miles of pipe, bringing clean water to villages all over the world, including Africa. "Africa is not water deficient," Wang has said. "It's infrastructure deficient."⁴ There is enough water available, but the means to get it to the people is lacking. One year Wang's company shipped over two hundred miles of pipe to seven African countries, providing 150,000 people with clean water. The villagers no longer had to walk miles to contaminated water sources. Public taps in the villages now provide clean, safe water a few steps from their homes.

As his company continues to grow, Wang believes God has placed him in his leadership position to not just pipe in physical water to people. He said God is also using him to funnel in "living water" to communities, as he shares the Gospel and tells others about God's miraculous saving grace.

A Mission on the Airwaves

CBN (Christian Broadcasting Network) was the first Christian television station in the United States. It began broadcasting on October 1, 1961. Now fifty years later, it is the largest television ministry in the world. It was founded by televangelist Dr. M.G. (Pat) Robertson, and its headquarters and main studio are in Virginia Beach, Virginia.

CBN utilizes a religious variety program format that has been successfully used in religious broadcasting ever since.[1] Today CBN programs have been seen in 108 languages and in 218 different countries and territories.

One of the mainstays of the network is *The 700 Club*. Originally the show refused commercial advertisements and was funded by 700 contributors donating ten dollars per month, hence its name. At the time, $7,000 was enough to allow CBN to meet its monthly expenses.

Today the network's journalistic branch, CBN News, provides news updates for *The 700 Club* and produces religious news programs such as *CBN News Watch* and *Christian World News*. The hour long talk-show *700 Club Interactive* is seen on the ABC Family channel. CBN is also the first Christian ministry to build and operate its own satellite. [2]

Additionally, CBN manages the Operation Blessing International Relief and Development Corporation. It is a nonprofit, humanitarian affiliate organization that Pat Robertson founded in 1978. It provides disaster relief, medical aid, hunger relief, orphan care, water wells and community development in Africa, Asia, Europe, Latin America, Haiti and the United States. CBN also produces programs for Indonesia, Thailand, India, Latin

American and British audiences and has broadcast programs in over seventy languages.

Pat Robertson founded Regent University, located in Virginia Beach, VA, in 1977, serving as its president and chancellor. The university is considered one of the nation's leading academic centers for Christian thought and action. It offers many graduate and undergraduate programs that are available worldwide. It is a fully accredited graduate university and has an enrollment of over four thousand. Their Worldwide Campus also offers programs online.

CBN's mission statement includes the following declarations:

"The mission of CBN and its affiliated organizations is to prepare the United States of America and the nations of the world for the coming of Jesus Christ and the establishment of the Kingdom of God on earth. Our ultimate goal is to achieve a time in history when 'the knowledge of the Lord will cover the earth as the waters cover the sea.' In achieving our mission nothing should be done that does not glorify God and His Son, Jesus Christ."[3]

THE TEA LADY

Eileen Hadaway is known as the "Tea Lady". She loves drinking tea, especially each morning as she reads her Bible with a cup in hand, spending time with the Lord. One day during her prayer time, she received an idea of how she could spread God's Word to others by putting a scripture verse on a tea tag. Thus was born the Scripture Tea Company.

Trying to get the business going was difficult, and money was not readily available from personal funds to make a large investment. Each tea bag had a Scripture verse on the tag and only quality tea and packaging were used. One morning, as she was reading scripture and looking for guidance, God led her to the Bible verse, Luke 6:38: *"Give, and it will be given to you. They will pour into your lap a good measure—pressed down, shaken together, and running over. For by your standard of measure it will be measured to you in return."*

So, the Hadaways decided to start giving tea away. Operation Blessing, sponsored by CBN (Christian Broadcasting Network), was chosen to receive the donation, because they so admired the work the organization does to help people during emergency times.

Eileen and her husband sent Operation Blessing thousands of tea bags. It wasn't too long before their business began to take off. Among the businesses that ordered and sold their product were Lifeway Christian Stores and Cracker Barrel. The Hadaways continued donating tea to Operation Blessing and became partners with the CBN project.

The first year saw their business double; then it tripled the second year! They give all of the credit for their success to God.

Each box of Scripture Tea carries the following message: "My desire through Scripture Tea is to not only give you a 'taste' of God's Word, but more importantly to give you a hunger to have more of His love and comfort by turning to the Bible for guidance. May God richly bless you, and all those to whom you choose to bless with Scripture Tea".[1]

HOLY LAND EXPERIENCE

The Holy Land Experience is located in Orlando, Florida. It was founded by Marvin Rosenthal and his son, David, and opened its doors to the public on February 5, 2001.[1]

Rev. Rosenthal was a Baptist pastor in the northeast, who had converted from Judaism to Christianity. He and his son, David, had been thinking about a religious theme park for years, and in 1989 they began the journey to make their dream a reality.

What follows is the story Marvin Rosenthal told an audience when my wife and I visited the Holy Land Experience in March of 2002.

Rosenthal felt a strong call to Florida where he planned to start a new ministry called Zion's Hope, a Protestant and Fundamentalist Christian non-profit organization. Along with this Rosenthal also felt a call from the Lord to find a unique approach to teach the Word of God in a way that would provide an experience of the historical, cultural and geographical setting of Bible times.

The idea of a miniature Holy Land theme park came to the forefront. He planned to create a park where everyone could experience the sights and sounds of the city of Jerusalem.

A real estate agent chauffeured Rosenthal and his son around looking at potential sites in the Orlando area. The agent talked price in terms of the dollar cost per foot of frontage. Rosenthal thought he meant dollars per acre! For example, the agent would say, "This property is 15". Rosenthal thought he meant the whole acreage would sell for around $15,000! Once the agent realized that the Rosenthals didn't have millions to spend, he lost interest in working with them.

Rosenthal's son suggested that they look at a prime piece of land where two major highways cross one another. They found a nineteen-acre patch of land in Orlando, located off Interstate 4 about five miles east of Universal Studios. Though the land was considerably more expensive than what they felt was reasonably within their sights, they made a bid of faith. What they didn't know was that the current owners of the land were going through a bankruptcy. The bankruptcy judge accepted Rosenthal's bid of $1.2 million. Now all they had to do was find the money to make the down-payment!

Rosenthal's telephone pleas for help from friends resulted in the necessary funds coming through for the down payment. Now money was needed to hire architects, arrange to get the necessary zoning and proceed to construction. Again, they went ahead on faith and prayer. Another supporter rescued the project by arranging for loans to fund and complete the project. The Holy Land Experience theme park became a reality.

They were ready to open the doors to the public, but now lacked the money to advertise!

The Holy Land Experience theme park had provoked criticism from local rabbis and other Jewish leaders who were concerned about the use of Jewish symbols and prayers in a Christian theme park. They also felt the park was created to try to convert Jews to Christianity. The Los Angeles-based Jewish Defense League promised to picket the opening and predicted two hundred people would participate.

Rosenthal and the theme park organization denied and refuted any plans to use profits to convert Jews to Christianity. The picket threat and accusations by the Jewish Defense League resulted in media coverage from around the world to cover the picketing. Only four picketers actually showed up. But the whole action provided plenty of free publicity for the theme park!

Before welcoming its first visitors, Rosenthal prayed for the Lord's protection of the Christian attraction. The park can be described as a living museum that authentically recreates the city of Jerusalem and its religious importance between the years of 1450 B.C. and 66 A.D.

On the first day many church groups, students and visitors streamed through the turnstiles at the main entrance, which is a life-sized replica of the Jerusalem gate. Visitors then enter into a marketplace, created to look like the one where Jesus walked through nearly two thousand years ago. The re-creations of the city are very realistic, and there are several high-tech presentations with special effects. Staff and characters in productions are all dressed in biblical costumes.

Just after noon on the first day the park reached capacity. Officials had to turn visitors away. Operations at the park had planned to accommodate eight hundred guests at one time, and there were one hundred eighty parking places for cars and buses. By mid-afternoon, officials said, nearly two thousand people had passed through the gates of the park!

In addition to the original park, the Holy Land Experience now includes an 18,000 square foot Scriptorium—a Center for Biblical Antiquities. It has a non-sectarian library and research center and is one of the most unique facilities of its kind in the world. It houses the world's finest collection of authentic biblical artifacts and antiquities, including ancient cuneiform, scrolls, rare manuscripts and Bibles. Many of these are the only known copies in existence.

Today the Holy Land Experience is supported by the Trinity Broadcasting Network and headed by Paul and Jan Crouch.

You can to read more about the theme park at www.theholylandexperience.org.

DaySpring Cards

DaySpring Cards was founded in 1971 in Covina, California, by four Christian men, Dean Kerns, Don Leetch, Russ Flint, and Roy Lessin. Their first printing endeavor was done on a printing press in Don Leetch's garage! The first card carried this simple Christmas message: "When you get right down to it . . . the only thing that really matters is Jesus."[1]

They had a common vision to use printed messages to make Christ and the Word more widely known. They took the company name from the King James Version of the Bible of Luke 1:78-79, which says: *"Through the tender mercy of our God; whereby the Dayspring from on high hath visited us, to give light to them that sit in darkness and in the shadow of death, to guide our feet into the way of peace."* (Dayspring is another name for Jesus.)

During their first eight years in California the company experienced great growth, and in 1979 the company was moved to Siloam Springs, Arkansas. Here the DaySpring plant was built in a lovely country setting along the Illinois River. Shortly after the move, DaySpring became a full-service greeting card company with distributions in Christian bookstores. This resulted in tremendous growth and success, and they became the largest publisher and distributer of Christian greeting cards in the world.

Further acquisitions and success continued, and they became partners with David C. Cook Publishing Company in 1987, followed by an acquisition by Hallmark Cards from Cook Communications in 1999.

In 2006 DaySpring founded another company. It was a company called Blessings Unlimited, which is a home party company offering Christian and inspirational products for sale by independent consultants. Entrepreneurs from across the USA sell these products and operate their own ministry-based business.

The DaySpring mission statement is as follows:

> "To KNOW GOD, to demonstrate His Kingdom, and to HELP PEOPLE throughout the world know and share HIS LOVE by providing Christians with TOOLS of communication that express GOD'S HEART in fresh, new ways."[2]

DaySpring strives to make community involvement and charitable giving a crucial part of their corporate mission. A local, national and international ministry is supported each year. The ministries to be served are chosen by a team of employees. The company then matches the donations made by the employees. Additionally, DaySpring gives employees two paid days per year as recognition of the time they spend as volunteers to local ministries.[3]

DaySpring donates greeting cards to ARM (American Rehabilitation Ministries). Through this endeavor over fifty million greeting cards have been distributed to prisons and jails across the nation. This is just another way of making Christ known in the lives of people who need to know the Lord.

You can find out more about the company at www.DaySpring.com.

MARKETPLACE CHAPLAINS

Marketplace Chaplains USA provides Chaplain Care Teams in corporate workplaces. They serve both public and private companies.[1] The company was started in Dallas, Texas, in 1984, with one Chaplain, the Founder and CEO, Gil A. Stricklin. He began his work with just one company of one hundred and fifty employees. The home office of Marketplace Chaplains USA is now located in Plano, Texas.

Today Marketplace Chaplains USA has a team of 2,500 male, female and ethnically diverse Chaplains. They work with hundreds of companies representing many different industries as diverse as banks, automobile dealerships, food processors, real estate firms, construction and trucking companies, law firms, restaurants, manufacturers and wholesale companies. Their work takes them to more than two thousand locations, located in forty-four states as well as two dozen international cities in Mexico, Puerto Rico, Europe and Canada. They work with companies that have only one employee and those that have several thousand employees. Marketplace Chaplains USA provides services to over 500,000 employees and family members.[2]

Their mission statement says:

"Marketplace Chaplains USA exists to share God's love through corporate chaplains in the workplace by an Employee Care Service for our corporate client companies, both in the United States of America and abroad."[3]

The chaplains visit the worksite on a regular basis, usually weekly. This helps to build a trusting relationship with the employees. Visits are on a voluntary basis. Contact can be as brief as a greeting and a handshake, to a more lengthy conversation about a family or health problem, a wedding, funeral, etc. An appointment can be made for discussion off site and off company time if necessary or desired.

Chaplains are on call 24/7, so they are available for emergencies even during the middle of the night. They provide visits to hospitals, nursing homes, funeral homes or jails. They are certified to perform weddings and conduct funerals. When deemed necessary, the chaplains may refer employees to other agencies and organizations to help with a specific need. All of the services provided to employees are available to family members of employees as well.

God makes His Word available even in the workplace!

GOD'S OTHER WAYS

God is making sure His master plan for the world from creation to eternity is realized. Only He knows how and when it will be completed. Each of us is only a tiny piece of the puzzle. Our perspective of time involves only moment to moment, day to day, within the limits of our lifetime. We may never know when something that happens today is an important part of a plan to be completed in the future. God has planned it and views it all from the perspective of eternity.

To help complete His plan, God uses numerous OTHER WAYS to make sure His Word is spread around the world. He instills in the hearts and minds of those who believe in Him the importance of getting the Message out to others.

Some take this on as professionals trained in the Word, like the stories of those who have felt a call to serve. Yet, anyone can also spread the word in a way that he or she is uniquely qualified. Many times this starts out as a strong, inward faith. Then events in people's lives lead them (with God's guidance) to share their faith in ways they never would have dreamed they would or could.

These next stories describe events that have blessed, encouraged, saved and sustained people in more recent times than in the Bible. Several have been written by friends of the author, and are so noted. They illustrate how God has inspired people to utilize talents they never thought they had, resulting in far-reaching dissemination of God's Word to others. Many of these people would be amazed to know how that what happened many years ago is still bearing fruit in today's world.

God's love and intervening power are shown in these witnessing stories. They can't be explained away—they really happened.

POW Sustained by God's POWer

Congressman Sam Johnson is an American hero. He served in the U.S. Air Force for twenty-nine years and was a highly-decorated fighter pilot. It was during his 25th combat mission on April 16, 1966, over North Vietnam that his F-4 Phantom Air Force jet was shot down.

When he ejected from the aircraft, his right arm was broken in two places, his left shoulder dislocated, and his back broken. He couldn't use either arm. (Note: Johnson used to be right-handed but is left-handed now, because his right arm never totally healed—his captors kept breaking it.)

Shortly after he was captured, he was placed before a firing squad. As he faced them, Sam said. "Jesus, I love you." . . . Then he heard a "click, click, click . . ."[1] as one after another the guns aimed at him didn't fire. You may think that this was a miracle, but as Paul Harvey used to say, "And now, the rest of the story!"

The North Vietnamese borrowed from the North Koreans the technique of mental torture designed to soften up POWs before interrogation. One of the methods they used was a mock firing squad like the one set to fire at Sam. He spent the next seven years in captivity, forty-two months of that time in solitary confinement. They treated him like any other prisoner, terribly.

In his book *Captive Warriors—A Vietnam POW's Story* he relates how God sustained him through the long captivity of torture and pain, and the emaciation he endured. He subsisted on a diet of small portions of the rice and pumpkin soup they fed him. He was isolated from other prisoners in a three foot by nine foot cement cell with dirt, grime and filth. Sam was completely alone.

There were just bugs, spiders, flies, mosquitoes, an occasional rat and Sam.

Sam experienced great loneliness and could have given up in despair. Instead, he gave his all to the Lord—he put all his fears, anxieties and feelings of isolation into the Lord's hands. When he thought he could stand the isolation no longer, he felt the Lord's presence surround him. This gave Sam renewed strength and courage to go on. He became more and more resolved to resist the enemy and not give up.

As he became closer to God and focused on Him, Sam was surprised all that he could remember and recall, from Bible verses and stories learned as a child to hymns sung many years before. Even when the guards increased their patrols and vigilance and he was stopped from any communication with other POWs, Sam could still talk freely with God.

He knew God was with him every moment he spent alone in the constraint of the dark and filthy cell. He was certain God heard his prayers and provided the recall of those Bible stories and verses as he needed them to sustain and strengthen his trust in the Lord. He would need that trust in the long days and nights that he still had to experience.

During those seven years Sam was placed for lengths of time in wooden leg stocks followed by time in leg irons. He noticed that the swelling of his ankles would lessen after being in the leg stocks, so when the irons were put back on, they would be looser. He said prayers of thanks to God for that relief.

Because the prisoners could not see one another, they devised a way to communicate with each other by tapping a code on the wall. One time Sam tapped a message asking who could name all sixty-six books of the Bible. To his surprise, he himself remembered all of them. He was even able to recall some of the book groupings, like the Pentateuch, major and minor prophets, etc.

The prison authority thought they could upset the prisoners' communication system by moving prisoners around and mixing them up. Instead they actually improved it. Each one trained another prisoner to use the special tapping code they had devised. They never saw one another nor knew what other prisoners looked like except maybe through a crack in a door. In case he ever got out of prison and back home, Sam committed to memory several hundred names of other POWs. He did this just by tapping the code on the wall.

Sam relates that one day a typhoon storm raged. A nearby river overflowed its banks, and he watched the water pour into his cell. He was standing on the slab which was about two feet higher than the floor. He pleaded with God to save him and the others. Night fell and gradually the rain began to stop. The next morning Sam looked out his cell's small, barred window and saw a marvelous sight—an absolutely perfect rainbow! He knew God had meant it for him. Sam said, "I see it Lord . . . . Your promise."[2]

Answers to his prayers surprised Sam in other ways, too. Unknown to the prisoners, negotiations for their release were taking place and they began to be treated more humanely. In addition to the improved treatment, the prisoners were fed better food, along with hot, fresh French bread. When Sam was captured, he weighed 190 lbs. His lowest weight in captivity was 120 lbs. As the time for his release drew nearer, the captors had fattened him up to about 150 lbs.

The POWs were also allowed to have worship on Easter, and then on other Sundays as well. Music and singing of Christmas carols and hymns followed. "I had seen the hand of God at work too often not to recognize His touch at this time. For me, all these things were more evidence of God's great grace."[3]

Despite his hesitation to do so, Sam often led the singing. The men sang *Silent Night*, followed by the *Battle Hymn of the Republic, The Star Spangled Banner, God Bless America*, etc.

It may not have been like the voices of a trained choir, but to the men it was beautiful and meaningful. Sam wrote in his book, "I felt a surge of victory inside. The American spirit had not been crushed. Years of captivity, torture, and starvation had not destroyed the souls of the nearly 350 American POWs in Camp Unity. Our bodies might be mangled and scarred, but our spirits remained intact."[4]

Sam says he felt like that without God by his side he never would have made it. He said he thought of his family all the time and hoped they were okay. His wife, Shirley, didn't know for two and a half years that he was anything but MIA—missing in action. Finally she was told that Sam was a POW. He was released from captivity on February 12, 1973.

Sam retired after nearly thirty years of service in the Air Force. He earned two silver stars, a distinguished flying cross, two purple hearts, four air medals and two legions of merit. Between the Korean and Viet Nam wars he was a "top gun" and flew with the Thunderbirds precision flying team in an F100C Sabre in both the solo and slot positions. When the six airplanes fly as a team the wing tips of the planes are as close as eighteen to thirty-six inches apart.

Sam relates in his book, "Years later I learned that Buzz (Aldrin—with whom Sam had shared a number of combat missions in North Korea), had thought of me during his flight into space to the moon. He had looked down on Southeast Asia from thousands of miles above the earth's atmosphere and wondered if I was still alive . . . . if I would ever make it home again. His first book, *Return to Earth,* dedicated to his wife, included a thought for me as well. My eyes blurred when I saw it for the first time and read the words: 'for Sam . . . . whose place I took, who took my place . . . .'"[5]

Surely God sustained Sam Johnson. He is currently serving as a United States Congressman from the 3rd District in Texas.

One of Sam's favorite scripture verses is Isaiah 40:29-31: *"He gives strength to the weary, and to him who lacks might He increases power. Though youths grow weary and tired, and vigorous young men stumble badly, yet those who wait for the Lord will gain new strength; They will mount up with wings like eagles, they will run and not get tired, they will walk and not become weary."*

Miracles, Prophecy and God's Other Ways

SHE SAVED SIX YEARS TO BUY A BIBLE

Mary Jones wanted a Bible of her own.[1] With persistence and even under difficult circumstances, she prevailed and got one.

Her fervor inspired the founding of the British and Foreign Bible Society and the global network it now encompasses. Its stated vision is: "We are working to see a day when the Bible's God-given revelation, inspiration and wisdom is shaping the lives and communities of people everywhere."[2]

Mary was born in 1784 into a poor family in Wales. Her parents were Calvinistic Methodists, and Mary became a Christian when she was eight years old. She learned to read at a school organized by Thomas Charles, who was a preacher from Bala, a town about twenty-five miles from where Mary lived. She often visited a farm some two miles from her home to read the Bible that was there. But, she had a burning desire to own a Bible of her own in her own language.[3]

Her hope seemed in vain, as there was little money and Bibles were hard to come by. It was not certain one would even be available for sale. Despite the slim hope, Mary saved her money. It took her six years before she had enough saved up to buy her own Welsh Bible. She heard that she might be able to buy one from Thomas Charles in the town of Bala. So, in 1800, at the age of fifteen, she set out and walked barefoot for twenty-five miles across valleys, streams and around mountains to Bala.

She came to the home of Reverend Charles, only to find out that all of the copies that he had were either sold or promised to others. Mary wept and was very distraught and heartbroken. Reverend Charles was touched by her devotion, and finally agreed to sell her one of the copies that he had promised to someone else.

It was the impression that Mary left on Reverend Charles that compelled him to make a proposal to the Council of the Religious Tract Society. He proposed they form a new Society for the purpose of supplying Bibles to the Welsh people. As a result The British and Foreign Bible Society was established in London in 1804.

Mary Jones died in 1864. The Bible she walked so far for is kept in the British and Foreign Bible Society archives located in the Cambridge University Library.[4] Two centuries later the worldwide work of the Society still continues and emphasizes the importance and relevance of God's Word for today.

MY HERO

Perhaps you've read the poem entitled *"One Solitary Life"*.[1] The author is unknown. It has many versions. Here is one of them:

> "He was born in a stable in an obscure village.
> From there He traveled less than 200 miles.
> He never won an election. He never went to College.
> He never owned a home. He never had a lot of money.
> He became a nomadic preacher. Popular opinion turned against Him.
> He was betrayed by a close friend, and His other friends ran away.
> He was unjustly condemned to death, crucified on a cross among common thieves,
> On a hill overlooking the town dump. And when dead, laid in a borrowed grave.
> Nineteen centuries have come and gone. Empires have risen and fallen.
> Mighty armies have marched and powerful rulers have reigned.
> Yet no one has affected men as much as He. He is the central figure of the human race.
> He is the Messiah, the Son of God, JESUS CHRIST!"

One morning I felt a compelling urge to rush to the computer and write what follows.

The words spilled out faster than I could write. It took me all of five minutes to write an updated version.

"My Hero"
by Kenneth R. Kersey

He doesn't wear a suit and tie to work.
He's not a whiz on Wall Street.
He doesn't own a lap top computer or have a cell phone.
He doesn't drive a fancy car.
He's not a movie star.
Nor does He have a TV show.
He's not a CEO that jets around the world.
Nor did He receive a single vote in the last election.
He doesn't live in a big house or fancy neighborhood;
He's never taken a vacation or a cruise.
He's never written a book nor had His picture taken.
The post office doesn't even have His address.
Yet, painters have portrayed Him.
Authors write about Him; Movies depict Him.
No one has affected men as much as He.
Twenty centuries have come and gone,
Wars are still fought in HIS name.
Politicians and presidents fade into history.
Friends who denied knowing Him,
Changed their minds and died for Him.
He is the central figure of the human race
He is the Messiah, the Son of God.
JESUS CHRIST!

I decided to have 2¼ in x 3½ laminated cards printed with this poem. I leave one on the table in restaurants for the waitress, have mailed them in my Christmas cards, and have distributed them anywhere I can. On the back side of the card it reads:

Reasons the Bible is True
Jesus Christ is the Messiah—The Son of God

1. Gospels and books in the New Testament were written by eyewitnesses to both the crucifixion and resurrection.
2. A Roman Guard, consisting of 4-16 Roman soldiers under penalty of death if a prisoner escaped, was posted to guard Jesus' tomb, and they did not refute the resurrection.
3. A stone weighing 1½ tons sealed the tomb. Could a crucified Jesus, encased by 100 lbs of spices, and in a tomb with a Roman seal and guard, roll away the stone and escape? Christ left empty cocoon-like grave clothes.
4. After the resurrection Jesus appeared to hundreds who confirmed His resurrection. If not true, many would have said so.
5. Eleven disciples (all cowards) became "flamingly" dedicated and died horrible deaths defending their belief in Jesus as the Messiah. People die for a cause they believe in. If Jesus was not resurrected, their cause died too.
6. Archaeological discoveries verify the accuracy of New Testament manuscripts.
7. Psalm 22 describes crucifixion 600+ years before it was first used.
8. To refute the resurrection claim the authorities only needed to produce Jesus' body, and they didn't, because they couldn't.
9. Apostle Paul (Saul of Tarsus) turned from persecuting Christians to following Christ. He died horribly for his belief.

I have also printed other cards with the following:

Things We Can't See But Know Exist

GRAVITY—We experience the effects of it.
HEAT and COLD—We can feel them.
SOUND—We can't see it, but we can hear it.
WIND—We feel breezes, and we can't live without air.
EMOTIONS—We feel the effects of love, hate, etc.
POWER—We experience the effects of energy.
LIFE—We know when something is alive.
TASTE—We experience salt, sour, and sweetness.
SMELL—We enjoy the scent and aroma of flowers.
RADIO, TV/CELL PHONE WAVES—We connect to others.
THOUGHTS and IMAGINATION—We all have them.
MAGNETISM—It attracts and repels, but we can't see it.

Likewise, GOD exists although we can't see HIM!

"The heavens are telling of the glory of God; and their expanse is declaring the work of His hands" (Psalm 19:1).

"Now faith is the assurance of things hoped for, the conviction of things not seen" (Hebrews 11:1).

"... for the things which are seen are temporal, but the things which are not seen are eternal" (2 Corinthians 4:18b)

Therefore ... there is no excuse for not believing in GOD!

THE BIBLE IN 14 WORDS!

God Created
Genesis 1:1

Man Disobeyed
Genesis 3:16

Jesus Saved
John 3:11b-13

Jesus Will Return, Judge and Rule for Eternity
Revelation 19:11-16

****

300 Old Testament Predictions Prophesy of Christ's First Coming

Jesus fulfilled *ALL* of these predictions

350 New Testament Predictions Prophesy of Christ's Second Coming

SALVATION IS A *FREE* GIFT
BELIEVE
AND
RECEIVE ETERNAL LIFE!

Isaiah 55:11 states,

> "So will My word be which goes forth from my mouth;
> It will not return to Me Empty, without accomplishing what I desire, and without succeeding in the matter for which I sent it."

The distribution of these laminated cards is another way of spreading God's Word. It may reach only a small audience, but God's Word is never spread and never said without accomplishing the purpose God planned for it.

Warned to Escape from Hiroshima

This story is related in a book written by Douglas Connelly called *Angels Around Us: What the Bible Really Says*.[1]

Mutsuko Hasegawa of Hiroshima, Japan, was brought to Christ by a missionary named Mabel Francis. Mutsuko hoped to become a missionary like her teacher, but a pre-arranged marriage by her family to a non-Christian man prevented that from happening.

Mutsuko and her husband had three daughters. When World War II broke out, her husband joined the emperor's army. He was killed in battle, and she was devastated to the point of considering suicide. Then the Lord spoke to her and reminded Mutsuko of her desire to become a missionary. Perhaps she could raise her daughters to be missionaries also.[2]

She got her life back on track, but then sensed that God was speaking to her again. She heard: "Escape to the mountain, escape to the mountain."[3] She heard this over and over again. Finally, Mutsuko and her three daughters packed up their belongings, hired a vehicle, and left the city of Hiroshima.

The next morning at 8:16 a.m. she watched from the safety of the mountains as a blinding flash and a mushroom cloud covered the city below her. The atomic bomb had been dropped by the United States on Japan.

This brings to mind the story in the Old Testament (Genesis 19) about Lot and his family. Just like the Lord led Lot's family from danger, He led Mutsuko and her daughters to safety from the destruction of the city they had left behind.

Mutsuko and her daughters were spared, and she realized her dream of becoming a missionary.

SEIZE ANY CHANCE TO PRAY

Dr. Jerry Cain, the president of Judson University in Elgin, Illinois, relates this story about a time he was driving across Oklahoma.[1]

"There wasn't a lot to see out the windshield during the trip, and I had listened to enough Huntley Brown and Johnny Cash so that I was ready for a break. As the red indicator on the gas gauge got close to "E", I pulled into a nondescript service station to refuel and stretch my legs.

"There was no one else within eyeshot, no cars were moving, and the horizon was bare. The only person anywhere close was a young lad inside the service station fretting over a pile of papers. After topping off the tank, I walked into the service station and asked to borrow a map. It cost $4.95 to buy one, and I just needed to check some road numbers for free. The lad smiled and pointed me to the map rack, thus giving me permission to borrow the information from Rand McNally, knowing I would pay for it some other time.

"After checking my route, I refolded the map correctly and put it back in the rack. I thanked the lad for his generosity and simply asked, 'Since I have to drive for another hour and have nothing else to do, how can I pray for you?'"

He looked a little relieved and bewildered at the same time as he cogitated on his options. Then I noticed the paperwork that was consuming his energies. He was working on the FAFSA (Free Application for Federal Student Aid), trying to fill out financial aid forms for college.

"I don't know much about history, don't know much biology and I don't remember much about the French I took in school, but because I work at a university I do know about FAFSAs. I spent the next twenty minutes explaining the process to him and helping him understand what numbers needed to go in what blanks. He was relieved, and by the time we finished the project, he was giggling. He commented, "You are a God-send." Inwardly I affirmed his evaluation.

"No one in his family had ever gone to college before and he was trying to complete the paperwork on his own. My stop at that gas station was the angelic visit which gave him direction and courage to keep going. I left my business card and received a note from him several months later. He was now in school in Oklahoma because of help on the FAFSA.

"God works in strange ways, in odd opportunities and consistently to advance His Kingdom. I am glad I could be a part of that."

Plant His Word, He Will Grow It

Chuck Swindoll is the senior pastor of Stonebriar Community Church in Frisco, Texas. He also has a daily Bible-teaching radio ministry, *Insight for Living*, which many have listened to since 1977. The program is now broadcast worldwide and can be heard in sixteen languages on more than 2,100 radio stations.

Chuck, as he is often called, had planned to become a mechanical engineer. While serving in the Marines in Okinawa in the 50s, he felt the call to the ministry.[1] He has shared this story from the pulpit, as well as on *Insight for Living*.

Chuck's bunk mate in Okinawa was named Eddie. When Eddie found out Chuck was a Christian, he told "Swindle" right off that he had no wish to be evangelized and Chuck should back off. As he reclined in the top bunk, Chuck would read the Bible and review the verses he was committing to memory. He tried to think of some way he could interest Eddie in learning about the Lord Jesus.

One day he handed Eddie some of his verse cards and asked Eddie to help him go over the words. This was repeated many times with dozens of verses. Most were about the Gospel and salvation, for example, John 3:16. Chuck would start saying the verse and intentionally hesitate at key words, which then prompted Eddie to give him the word to continue. This went on and on, over and over again.

It was about thirty years later that Chuck received a phone call. On the other end, someone said, "Hey, Swindle!" He knew immediately it had to be Eddie. Eddie said to him, "Hey, you know that trick you played on me in Okinawa? Well, it worked! I'm loving Jesus now!"[2]

This speaks of the power of God and the sure and eventual completion of the plans He has. As is stated in Isaiah 55:10-11, *"For as the rain and the snow come down from heaven, and do not return there without watering the earth and making it bear and sprout, and furnishing seed to the sower and bread to the eater; so will My word be which goes forth from My mouth; it will not return to Me empty, without accomplishing what I desire, and without succeeding in the matter for which I sent it."*

Dr. Swindoll served as pastor of churches in Texas, Massachusetts and California before returning to Texas in 1994 to become the president of Dallas Theological Seminary. He and a group of fellow believers established the non-denominational Stonebriar Community Church in 1998. Additional information on Chuck's ministries can be found at www.stonebriar.org and www.insight.org.

TRIALS STRENGTHEN HER FAITH

This next story is written by one of my Christian friends, Kay Young.[1] Kay has endured many physical trials in her lifetime, yet her strong faith in the Lord Jesus radiates with joy in all that she says and does. This is her testimony.

"I had a God-fearing mother who taught my sister and me about the Lord. I was a stinker growing up and my high school years were tumultuous, but I got through them pretty well. Several years later I met my husband, Jim Young. We got married and have three kids, Ronda, Jim Jr. and Dan. God was good to me. He surrounded me with family, a strong praying church, and friends. This support team helped me to go through the "various trials" that happened next.

"In 1978 I had breast cancer. In 1982 I had a brain tumor, and in 1997 I had lymphoma. So, I'm a three-time cancer survivor. I want to tell you about one of my ordeals and how our amazing and awesome God changed our lives forever.

"In February, 1982, I was walking in a store, and my left shoe kept coming off. Within a few days my left knee was buckling, and I had to walk with a crutch. I finally decided to go to my doctor, but I couldn't get in to see him for another two weeks. At that visit he referred me to an orthopedic surgeon. This doctor felt that it wasn't my knee, but that it could be in my back or my neck. He referred me to a neurosurgeon.

"I called the neurosurgeon's office not expecting to get an appointment for weeks or months. It was a Friday afternoon, and I couldn't imagine getting in to see any doctor, much less a specialist. But in God's providence, I was told the doctor had a cancellation, and could I come right then!!!

"The doctor ran some tests. First, he lifted my arms with my eyes closed, then had me lie on my stomach and lifted my feet and told me to hold them up. My left arm and left leg were dropping, but I didn't realize it. My mind was spinning, because I had seen this exact thing on television many years earlier. I thought, 'He thinks I've got a brain tumor!!!'"

"The doctor wanted to run some additional tests that required me to be admitted to the hospital. I entered the hospital the following week.

"The first test was a CAT scan. After the initial scan, I heard the tech ask the assistant to call the doctor—there was something on the scan. Well, I was wide awake now for sure. Then she told me she needed to rescan a few areas. The doctor came in almost running. He said that there was something in my brain, and he had to get it out. Surgery was scheduled for the next week.

"Up to this point, we had not told the kids anything. But we now had good information to give them that they could understand. They were clearly scared—but then, so were we. We prayed together as a family and afterward we all felt comforted.

"We were members of the Ambassador Class at Northwest Bible Church in Dallas. When Jim told them I had a brain tumor, all the prayer chains kicked into high gear. They prayed for a miracle, healing for me and strength for Jim and the kids, but most of all, for God's will.

"The evening before surgery, we had a gathering in my hospital room. Family and friends were there. We prayed, we laughed, and we talked about what a great God we have. Then Jim and I spent some time alone. We needed that time together.

"I knew there was the possibility that my left side could be paralyzed after the surgery, and I was okay with that. I just wanted to live and take care of my husband and kids. I would learn how to manage. What I didn't know before the surgery was that the doctor had told Jim that without the surgery, I might live three months; with the surgery, I might make it to Christmas.

"That night I had trouble sleeping; I got my Bible and read from Psalm 139:1-4.

> *'O Lord, You have searched me and known me, You know when I sit down and when I rise up; You understand my thought from afar. You scrutinize my path and my lying down, and are intimately acquainted with all my ways. Even before there is a word on my tongue, Behold, O Lord, you know it all.'*

"Pretty amazing God!!

"When Jim got to the hospital the next morning, he asked me how I had slept. I told him about my night. He said I should have called him. He was awake reading in the Bible also, James 1.

> *'Consider it all joy, my brethren, when you encounter various trials, knowing that the testing of your faith produces endurance. And let endurance have its perfect result, so that you may be perfect and complete, lacking nothing. But if any of you lacks wisdom, let him ask of God, who gives to all generously and without reproach, and it will be given to him'* (James 1:2-5).

"Now I was totally ready for whatever God had in store for me. I knew my/our lives would be changed forever, but with God on our side, we knew it would be okay.

"The surgery was expected to take about two hours. Instead it took nearly five hours! As you might imagine, all those who had gathered in the waiting room—about twenty-six persons—were anxious. Even the nurses on my floor were calling for updates!

"Finally the doctor came in and announced, "Kay might outlive us all!" He explained that he thought the tumor would come out easily. But, when he got in there, the tumor came apart, and he had to remove it piece by piece. That is why the surgery took so long. He was confident that he had gotten it all.

"He did explain that my left side was paralyzed because the golf-ball sized tumor was on a motor nerve, and he had to interrupt the nerve to get the entire tumor. He said other than that, with a lot of therapy, I would be able to live a normal life!

"A while later we received more great news. The doctor had sent all the lab work, tissue samples, test results, etc. to Duke University for study. The results from Duke were that the tumor was a malignant astro-cytoma, which can be terminal. The results also verified that the doctor had gotten it all, and no further treatment was needed!

"It is now 28+ years later since the brain tumor, and our life is good. God is a loving God, who puts His protective arms around me at home, when I drive, or wherever I am. I wouldn't be here were it not for the Lord. He has a great plan for my life, and I look forward to each and every day.

"I still deal with the challenges of having only one arm that works, and one pretty good leg, plus one paralyzed leg. I still have problems with my balance, and I have fallen a number of times. To help prevent falling, I have a balance and mobility dog. How I got him is another story about God's grace. He is a big golden retriever named Travis. I've had him for several years. If I fall here at the house, which has happened, he has his own phone. It is in our bedroom. He can bring the phone to me so I can call Jim, a neighbor or the paramedics.

"I want to leave you with a very special Scripture. In 2 Corinthians 12:9-10, Paul wrote:

> *'And He has said to me, 'My grace is sufficient for you, for power is perfected in weakness.' Most gladly, therefore, I will rather boast about my weaknesses, so that the power of Christ may dwell in me. Therefore, I am well content with weaknesses, with insults, with distresses, with persecutions, with difficulties, for Christ's sake; for when I am weak, then I am strong.'"*

GOD IS SOVEREIGN

Marjorie Dubert was a member of my fellowship class at church. Before her death in 2010, she e-mailed me this story.[1]

> "Whatever the Lord pleases, He does, in heaven and in earth, in the seas and in all deeps" (Psalm 135:6). "He, who is the blessed and only Sovereign, the King of kings and Lord of lords" (1Timothy 6:15).

"A very vivid lesson showing me that God is Sovereign occurred during my years of serving him in Papua New Guinea with Wycliffe Bible Translators/Summer Institute of Linguistics.

"LaVonne (Vonnie) was a fellow graduate student from Columbia Bible College in South Carolina. In the summer of 1954 she sang at my wedding. The next time I saw her was in early 1962. She was now Mrs. Walt Steinkraus doing Bible translation with her husband and children for the Tifalmin people in Papua New Guinea. They welcomed my husband and me with our children as fellow translators.

"In March of 1971 Vonnie came by our home at Ukarumpa to say good-bye. She and the two girls, Kerry 12, and Katherine 2, were off to a different village to join Walt. She could have left Kerry in the Children's Home to attend the International Primary School, but Kerry chose to go along to the village. Vonnie told me, "We want to glorify God as a family."

"Vonnie and the girls arrived in the new village on March 19. Two days later, on a beautiful sunny Sunday, the Steinkraus family attended church in a nearby village. They returned home and lay down to rest, while many in the village took the opportunity to work in their gardens or gather firewood. At 3:00 p.m., a freak landslide, a half-mile long, three hundred feet high and one hundred feet deep crossed the river and covered the village with terrific force. All in the village, including Vonnie and her family, died instantly.

"An envelope found in the debris had this verse written on it,

> 'For as the heavens are higher than the earth, so are My ways higher than your ways and My thoughts than your thoughts' (Isaiah 55:9).

"God raised up other Bible translators, Al and Susan Boush, to finish the translation project Walt and Vonnie Steinkraus had started. As a result the Tifalmin people now have the complete New Testament in their own language.

"Another missionary family, John and Bonnie Nystrom, had a close call but survived. They were doing Bible translation for the Arop people in Papua New Guinea. On July 17, 1998, an earthquake occurred a few miles off the shore of Arop. It caused three thirty-three foot high tsunamis to come ashore. All of the houses and many of the people in the Arop village at the time were swept out to sea. This included the home of the Nystroms. In the sovereignty of God, the Nystroms and their two children, along with all of their translation materials, were safe and sound at the Ukarumpa Center located nearby.

"God used the Nystrom family to give the survivors hope. The Nystroms chose additional translation helpers, and set up a training center where they now train and work with translators for eleven other languages as well as the Arop.

"I marvel at the mysterious hand of our Sovereign Lord and King. His ways are indeed higher than my ways. He chose to take the Steinkraus family, yet allowed the Nystrom family to remain, all the while furthering His Kingdom and glorifying Himself."

GOD USES WEATHER AND NATURE

I believe God has used weather and nature to intervene in history to make sure His plan for the world is fulfilled. Telling all these occurrences would be a book in itself. Therefore, I will relate only a few stories about events when weather was a major factor in the outcome.

Probably the most well-known Bible story where weather played a major role is the story of Noah's Ark and the flood, as told in the book of Genesis (Chapters 6-9). God warned mankind, *"I will blot out man whom I have created from the face of the land, from man to animals to creeping things and to birds of the sky; for I am sorry that I have made them"* (Genesis 6:7).

Before sending the flood, God commanded Noah to build a huge wooden ark with specific measurements. God's purpose for the flood was to destroy wickedness and sin. Noah was one righteous man among all the people of that time. His family, along with a menagerie of animals, was saved from the flood.

Some say that the flood was not world-wide and that the story was a parable. However, there are some two hundred cultures around the world that have in their history a record of a huge flood. The details are almost identical to the Bible's Noah story, and are recorded in Persian, Babylonian, ancient Egyptian, Chinese, and Sanskrit histories. A flood story is also related in the Koran.[1]

It was not until a discovery in 1872 made by George Smith, working in the British Museum, that written verification of the flood was made. Smith pieced together and translated 25,000 pieces of clay tablets from the *Epic of Gilgamesh*, which contained the Assyrian version of the flood story. The tablets had been unearthed near the ancient city of Nineveh.[2]

Another Bible story tells about the time God's chosen people had moved to Egypt to escape a famine in their land caused by lack of rain (Genesis 41-46). Over the years the Israelites multiplied in Egypt, but they became slaves to the Egyptians. God chose Moses to lead the people from Egypt to a land that he had promised Abraham many years before (Genesis 12:1-3, 14:14-16, and 17:7-9.) The Pharaoh of Egypt refused to let the Israelites go, so the Lord inflicted ten plagues on the Egyptian people to convince Pharaoh to release His people.

Horrible afflictions like infestations of frogs, lice, and locusts and a huge hailstorm were sent by God (Exodus 8-10). Still Pharaoh refused. When the tenth and last plague caused the first-born in every Egyptian family to die, Pharaoh finally agreed the Israelites could leave. Then he reneged on this decision and sent his army and chariots after the fleeing Israelites. God parted the waters of the Red Sea to provide an escape for the Israelites, and then sent a strong east wind to close the waters after the Israelites were on the other side. The pursuing Egyptian army was drowned, and the Israelites were safe from pursuit. (Exodus 14:21-28).

In the New Testament, Jesus calmed a storm on the Sea of Galilee (Luke 7:24). God used a storm to cause a shipwreck that stranded the Apostle Paul while on his way to Rome (Acts 27). There are many other examples of God's use of storms and weather in the Bible.

The Bible claims in Malachi 3:5 and Hebrews 13:8 that God is the same yesterday, today and tomorrow. God has continued to use His control of nature and the weather throughout history to accomplish His will. The following four stories are more examples of God's intervention using weather, but in more recent times.

How God Works in Today's World

Christopher Columbus

In 1492 Christopher Columbus sailed west from Spain on an expedition financed by Queen Isabella and King Ferdinand of Spain. Columbus was a Christian. In the book, *The Light and the Glory* by Peter Marshall and David Manuel, the authors say that Columbus felt called by God for his mission. Isaiah 49:1 and 6 state that God would cause events to occur so that His "salvation may reach to the end of the earth".[3]

After many days at sea Columbus' crew became restless and wanted to turn back. Columbus bargained with them. He agreed that if land was not sighted within three more days, he would turn around and go back to Spain. A strong wind came up and carried them further and faster than they had experienced for most of their journey. Then when four hours remained in the third and final day, land was finally sighted.

Columbus also discovered the West Indies, Central America, the Bahamas, Cuba and Haiti. The historical significance of Christopher Columbus' discoveries is tremendous. The world changed because of his voyages. The culture of Europe, along with its Christian religions, permeated the New World. Columbus did not find a new route to Asia as he planned. However, his discoveries did open the western hemisphere to colonization by the Europeans, who brought Christianity with them. His discovery altered the course of human history on a global scale.[4]

The War of 1812

The War of 1812 has been called "The Forgotten War", and has also been called "The Second Revolutionary War". America had won the first Revolutionary War thirty years earlier, but some of the British still looked on America as a weakling. The War of 1812 changed their perception.

President James Madison declared war on the British because they were boarding American ships and taking Americans prisoner. The British were using the American prisoners to help them carry on the war they were fighting with Napoleon in France.

In 1814 the White House along with other government buildings in Washington, D.C., were set on fire by the British when they stormed the city. God chose His own storms. Three tornadoes hit the city that day and caused a debacle for the British. Many British soldiers were injured or killed by the tornadoes. Upon leaving Washington, the British troops discovered that their ships moored in harbors nearby had been destroyed or washed ashore. It was a complete rout for the British. The violent and accompanying heavy rainstorms helped to extinguish the fires in the city. A tornado has rarely been seen in Washington, D.C. since.[5]

Also during the war of 1812, Andrew Jackson defended New Orleans. His troops hid behind a long barricade of dirt they had built between a canal and a dense forest. The barricade faced a meadow over which the British would have to cross to get to New Orleans. Jackson's troops waited. Heavy fog had settled on the meadow as the British started their march across it. Then suddenly the fog lifted and the British troops were exposed and vulnerable to attack. Jackson and his men won the battle.[6]

World War II

During World War II God used weather at a crucial moment in May of 1940 that changed the course of history. Hitler had defeated France and was marching on the Netherlands and

Belgium. The British army of 300,000 men was pushed toward Dunkirk, the only port they could go to in order to be evacuated. Their backs were to the English Channel.

God intervened. Hitler decided he would be too far from supply lines, so he stopped the advance of German tanks when they were just twenty miles from Dunkirk. Sudden heavy thunderstorms occurred that prohibited the Germans from flying their planes. Amazingly the sea stayed calm. This gave the British the opportunity to get to Dunkirk and start their sea evacuation. King George VI of England called for a National Day of Prayer for the troops and their efforts. As the evacuation progressed, the English Channel remained calm. The day after the evacuation, the seas became rough from a strong north wind and huge waves pounded the beaches they had just left.[7]

Normandy D-Day Invasion

God intervened with weather again during World War II in June, 1944, when the D-Day Invasion of Normandy took place.

The Germans were advised that the on-going stormy weather would preclude any invasion at that time. They were caught off-guard, when for a brief period the necessary weather conditions converged.

For the Allied invasion to succeed, the Army needed firm dry ground with no heavy rain. The Navy needed light winds and small waves for a prolonged period of time. The Air Force needed special cloud conditions for its bombers and fighter planes. In order to use gliders and drop paratroops, a clear moonlit night with no fog was required. The barometric pressure had to be nearly perfect to create these conditions.

General Eisenhower gave the go-ahead for the invasion. It involved 2,727 ships and nearly three million men, making it the largest and most powerful armada in world history. The Allied army faced fifty German divisions, and the steep cliffs at Omaha beach favored the German army.

Again God was in control. The invasion of Normandy succeeded, Europe was liberated, and Hitler defeated. "General Eisenhower knew that God had intervened at one of the most important moments in the history of the world!"[8]

> *"For the eyes of the Lord move to and fro throughout the earth that He may strongly support those whose heart is completely His"* (2 Chronicles 16:9).

Wordless Book and Bracelets

The creation of the Wordless Book is credited to the famous London Baptist preacher Charles Haddon Spurgeon.[1] On January 11, 1866, he was giving a message to several hundred orphans based on the verse, Psalm 51:7: *"Wash me, and I shall be whiter than snow."*

On that day the Wordless Book consisted of three pieces of paper colored black, red and white. Spurgeon used the book to share God's plan for salvation. Black symbolized sin; the red represented the blood of Christ shed on the cross; and the white page stood for the cleansing of sins received through the sacrifice made by Jesus Christ.

The Wordless Book and the Salvation Colors bracelet have proven to be a very easy and effective way to share the Gospel message. They are especially helpful in teaching the basic Gospel story to children, those who cannot read, or to people of different cultures. The book consists of pages of different colors, and the bracelets are made with colored beads. The colors can also be presented on a single page or as a banner.

In 1875 another pastor, D.L. Moody, began regularly using the Wordless Book in Liverpool, England. He added a gold page to represent heaven. Fanny Crosby (1820-1915), the beloved blind writer of hymns, used the Wordless Book with children.[2] She always carried one in her purse. The children would beg her to *read* the Gospel story over and over again.

In 1895, missionary Amy Carmichael used the Wordless Book to share the Good News in India. She made a satin flag with the colors of gold, black, red and white. The flag was attached to an ox-cart that she used for traveling from village to village.

She would tell the gospel story using the colors of the flag to the villagers and children.

A green page was added by Child Evangelism Fellowship (CEF) to represent growth in the Christian faith that is realized through reading and studying the Scriptures.

Here is a recap of the Colors of Faith, along with some appropriate Bible verses.[3]

Gold	reminds us of Heaven	Revelation 21:21
Black	reminds us of sin	Romans 3:23
Red	reminds us of Jesus' blood	Romans 5:8, John 3:16
White	reminds us of a clean heart	Psalm 51:7, Romans 10:9
Green	growing to know Jesus	2 Peter 3:18

Wordless books have evolved into many forms and everyday situations. The colors are displayed on wristbands, various sports gear and especially on soccer balls, basketballs, and volleyballs.

Sports gear and balls have proven to be very effective for use in evangelism. Sports can be an international language. Even in countries where television, radio, newspapers, and other modern communication means are rare, or where people cannot even read, soccer is played and there is an interest in sports.

Sports breaks down cultural and language barriers. When a player using a colored soccer ball is asked what the colors mean, a door is opened to talk about Jesus and the Gospel. The colors help to evangelize by starting conversations between people who don't know one another personally.

Teams of evangelists who play soccer have opened doors to the Gospel message in China. They are not allowed to openly evangelize, but they can answer questions. They often go to college campuses, where they gather a group to play a soccer game and use the multi-colored soccer ball.

Often they are asked about the colors on the ball, and this presents an opportunity to explain their meaning. When the game is over, the team leaves the soccer ball together with a pump, needle and tracts explaining the Gospel message in the language spoken and read in the country. Many East Asian cultures use color symbolism, making the use of the colors on the balls easily understood.

Many countries and cultures in the world ban religion, and their people suffer religious persecution. It is amazing that Christianity is still alive and growing. With all of the historical and ongoing criticism of Christianity through politics, censorship and persecution, one would think belief would be dying. But one-to-one contact to tell the Gospel is all that is needed. Sports evangelism accomplishes this and is another way that God continues to work in today's world.

The wordless bracelets have become so effective in evangelism efforts, that churches have Christian fellowship parties to make them for distribution. They are wonderful mission projects for youth and teens. All that is needed are the colored beads and leather strips which can be purchased at most handicraft stores. There are also web sites that give step by step directions.

"Permit the Children to Come to Me"

On their website, www.cefonline.com, Child Evangelism Fellowship (also known as CEF) states the following as their goal and mission: "Child Evangelism Fellowship is a Bible-centered, worldwide organization that is dedicated to seeing every child reached with the Gospel of the Lord Jesus Christ, discipled and established in a local church."[1]

Though CEF has many types of evangelism programs, one of the better-known is *The Good News Club.* These clubs are offered once a week after school in elementary school settings for children first through fifth grade by arrangements made with the local school district and the individual school.

The clubs present a fast-paced, one-hour program that is designed to present the Gospel to children on their level of understanding in a familiar place. Attendance is, of course, voluntary. Parents give their permission and support. The people who teach and work with the children are carefully-screened volunteer adults. No school supplies or staff members are used for the club.

Such clubs are established and operating in the Dallas, Texas, area. In one of the clubs, a ten year old girl in fourth grade (we'll call her Laurie) did what Christian adults in most of the United States hesitate to do. She proclaimed the Gospel of Jesus Christ to her peers. With her Christian faith strengthened by her home and church training as well as enrichment experienced in her *Good News Club,* she found the opportunity to explain the Gospel to her regular school class. Here is how it happened.

An assignment was given by Laurie's teacher for each student to present to the class an explanation about a topic others might not know about. One of the Muslim children in the class gave a lengthy presentation about the Muslim religion. Laurie and a friend in the class asked the teacher if they could work together on their presentation and tell the class about Christianity. The teacher gave them her permission.

Laurie and her friend produced a Power Point presentation with informative and descriptive displays and used it to tell the class about the Gospel and how Christianity can change lives. Of course, at the same time, they were also witnessing to both the teacher and the students!

Laurie and her friend love Jesus and they felt emboldened to share His love and grace with others.

The Bible says, *"Permit the children to come to Me, and do not hinder them, for the kingdom of God belongs to such as these"* (Luke 18:16).

Polio Makes Therapy Her Life's Work

This is a story from Donna McKinley, one of the therapy people I have worked with to strengthen and maintain my mobility. Like her, I also had polio as a young child. Donna sent this e-mail to me.

"I always knew that I had polio for a reason. God had plans for my life (Psalm 139:16, Jeremiah 29:11).

"I was two years old when I started therapy. I don't remember the therapist's face, but I do remember her hands. My parents had to drive to Waco, about sixty miles from my hometown, to take me to see the therapist. They did this every Saturday for two years. Even though we had family in Waco, we were not welcomed to stay at their home. They were afraid that their children would get the polio from me.

"My mother exercised my legs everyday on a large wooden box that was built for that purpose. It had a layer of quilts on it to make it soft. Then my mother died at age forty-four of a brain aneurysm. I moved to a much larger city where I started high school. When asked what I wanted to be, I always said that I wanted to be a physical therapist. I wanted to be like *the lady with the great hands.*

"I applied to enter a physical therapy program in Galveston. They received five hundred applications for only fifty positions. Mine was accepted! When I graduated, my husband and I moved to Austin. There I found work and put my husband through college.

"Since that time I have been at acute care hospitals, rehab hospitals, nursing homes, schools, outpatient clinics, and home health agencies. I consider myself a therapist who specializes in brain and spinal cord problems. I still see patients that have had polio as well. Recently I realized that God is guiding me during the treatments I give.

"It is said that God works through a doctor to help him help others! Well, he is working through me as well. I often dream that I am treating a difficult patient and one for which progress has been very slow or not expected. In my dream I am doing a treatment that I might not have thought of on my own. I don't always remember these dreams until I see the patient that I had the dream about. I try the treatment and it works!

"One time this happened when I was handling a very involved case with a young man who couldn't speak and had very little movement capability. He was known to be a Christian and was surrounded by church and friends who prayed for his recovery. I tried to do the exact treatment that I saw myself giving this young man in my dream.

"For the first time, he was able to help me roll him on his side and back. This happened, not once, but several times. Everyone was so excited that he had done this that it was posted on the internet!

"I believe I was given polio so I could help others and make a difference in their lives."[1]

Parachuting the Gospel

The Voice of the Martyrs (VOM) is a non-profit, interdenominational Christian organization. Their main purpose is to assist those around the world who are persecuted because they profess to be Christians. The ministry is based on Hebrews 13:3: *"Remember the prisoners, as though in prison with them and those who are ill-treated, since you yourselves also are in the body".*

The mission statement of VOM states, "We help Christians who are or have been, persecuted for their involvement in spreading the gospel of Jesus Christ. We provide medical assistance, food, clothing, and other forms of aid".[1]

Voice of the Martyrs (originally called Jesus to the Communist World) was officially started by Pastor Richard Wurmbrand in 1967. He and his wife were imprisoned for fourteen years in Communist Romania because of their faith in Christ. After they and their son were ransomed out of Romania, they came to the United States in the 1960s.

Pastor Wurbrand distributed the first monthly issue of *The Voice of the Martyrs* newsletter in the United States in October, 1967. The organization continues its monthly newsletter to this day. By the mid-1980s the work of VOM had been planted in eighty nations that restricted Christianity, and a network of VOM offices had been established around the world. All are for the sole purpose of assisting the persecuted church.

Wurbrand's book, *Tortured for Christ,* was released for publication in 1967. During his years of ministry he wrote eighteen books, some in English, others in Romanian. Several of them were translated into thirty-eight other languages. He retired from VOM in 1992. He then continued his devotion to the organization's work by serving as a consultant and member of the board of directors. Richard Wurbrand passed away in 2001.

Voice of the Martyrs is helping to spread the gospel message of Christ to the Marxist FARC Guerrillas in Columbia.[2] Since the 1960s there has been a war of terrorism between drug lords and paramilitary groups in that country. Caught in the middle are the people of Columbia, who have been terrorized by kidnappings and murders. Christians are risking their lives to spread the gospel there.

With the assistance of VOM a pilot in Columbia bought an airplane. He flies over the FARC-controlled territories and drops packages that are attached to parachutes. These packages include a selection of Christian books and a radio that is solar-powered. The radio is turned on and pre-tuned to a Christian radio station before the parachute is dropped. Even if the parachute gets caught in a tree, someone will be inclined to climb the tree to get it.

VOM says that many more of the FARC guerrillas need to hear the gospel. Churches around the world have helped by making more than 60,000 parachutes. A pattern showing how to make the parachutes can be downloaded from this website: www.persecution.com/parachute. Other information on the site gives details about VOM's work in Columbia, along with a video showing how guerrillas are being reached for Christ.[2]

In their 27th "Status of Global Mission" report, the *International Bulletin for Missionary Research* defines a martyr as "believers in Christ who have lost their lives, prematurely, in situations of witness, as a result of human hostility."[3] The report estimates that during the past decade (2000-2010), there were two hundred seventy new Christian martyrs every twenty-four hours. This makes the total number of martyrs in that decade approximately one million.[4] It has been estimated that there were forty-five million Christian martyrs during the twentieth century.[5] The World Evangelical Alliance has stated that more than two hundred million Christians in at least sixty countries are denied fundamental human rights solely because of their faith.[6]

Even with this data, it is impossible to know with certainty the number of Christians who are killed for their faith each year. Only heaven knows for sure. Much of the persecution takes place in remote areas unreachable by modern communications. Since persecution is often the norm in persecuted people's lives, they don't even think to tell others about what has happened to them and others. Most often they are afraid to do so.

There are many organizations that attempt to determine the number of martyrs. Voice of the Martyrs is another voice that aims their focus on people who are persecuted, helping where they can, and telling their stories so that others will also be stirred to help.

SHE MET GOD "IN THE GARDEN"

The following story was sent to me by Jeanelle Sims, who is a member of my fellowship class at church. She also teaches a small Bible study group at a local senior center in Little Elm, Texas. Here is her story![1]

"I walked down the aisle of a Baptist church when I was ten years old. All the others kids were walking down, too. As far as I was concerned I was joining the church. At the time, I had no idea what that meant, and I do not recall that anyone explained it to me. The years passed.

"My husband, James, and I had been married nine years. We had not been going to church nor had anyone come to visit us from a church. About two months before the *event*, I was Christmas shopping. I picked up a Living Translation Bible to use as a gift for someone. I thought, 'They sure could use it, but I never would.' Somehow I never gave it to anyone. As it turned out, the Lord would use it later—for me.

"The *event* happened at 9:30 a.m. on February 5, 1977. I was forty-seven years old, and I was BORN AGAIN! My rebirth happened this way!

"I was at home alone, and I felt the strong urge to kneel by my sofa. What happened next has always been a mystery to me. I don't know why God choose to set me free from all the guilt that had built up inside of me from the age of ten to age forty-seven.

In other words, a lot of dirty water had gone under the bridge during that time. He said that He has forgotten it. He gave me a hunger for His Word that has never left me. Praise The Lord!

"When I got up from my knees I knew that something had happened to me. I felt different. The guilt was lifted from me.

It was like the weight of a ten-ton rock had been lifted off my shoulders. I was different. I knew that God was real and not just some story that I had heard all my life. But, I was still not quite sure who Jesus was and what He had done for me. The Holy Spirit began to teach me about Jesus, and thus began my journey with the Lord.

"God woke me up every night at 2:00 am with scripture running through my mind and my hands up in the air praising Him. One night I thought that maybe I needed to get up and write the words down, and so I did.

"My husband, James, woke up and peeped around the corner. He asked what I was doing. I told him the Lord and I were writing a song. I began to tell him the lyrics. 'I come to the garden alone, while the dew is still on the roses'. James said, 'Does it go something like this?', and he began to sing it.

"Just because that hymn was written in 1912 by C. Austin Miles will never convince me that the Lord and I did not share that song, *In The Garden*, that night.[2] But, the important thing for sure is that He meant for me to understand that 'He walks with me and He talks to me and He tells me I am His own'. Now that's SECURITY!

"Over the last thirty-four years He has NEVER let me down. I will never stop praising Him. I praise Him for letting me live to see my children, grandchildren and great grand-children. He's given me the best husband in the world, who has put up with me for more than forty-two years.

"This is an on-going story. I'm not home yet."

(C. Austin Miles lived 1868-1948. He based his song, *"In the Garden"* on John 20: 11,15,16.)

Miners Saved Half Mile Underground

The Chilean mining accident happened on August 5, 2010, when a large cave-in occurred at the San Jose copper-gold mine located in northern Chile between the Andes Mountains and Pacific Ocean. Thirty-three men were trapped 2,300 feet underground about three miles from the entrance to the mine. They remained trapped there for sixty-nine days.

At first no one knew if they were alive or dead. Several attempts to bore exploratory holes with the hope of reaching them were unsuccessful. Then on the seventeenth day, just when the rescue team was close to giving up hope, a drill bit penetrated the cavity of the mine where the men were located. A note from the miners was attached to the drill bit, which said, "Estamos bien en el refugio, los 33". In English this translates to: "We are all well in the shelter, the 33".[1]

The rescue effort began and ultimately many nations and even NASA participated in the endeavor. A few days later one of the miners, Jimmy Sanchez, sent a letter up from the mine stating: "There are actually thirty-four of us, because God has never left us down here."[2] The miners' story is a testimony of their strong faith and God's amazing love and grace.

During the first seventeen days of their ordeal, with no contact with the outside world, they turned to Luis Urzua, the shift supervisor, to provide leadership and discipline. He is credited with keeping the men alive and in as good shape as they were when they were finally rescued.

The area they were in measured approximately five hundred square feet, about the size of a small studio apartment. The temperature was a humid 90°F, and the only source of light they had came from their helmet lamps. They kept these charged by using the battery from a work truck. The food available was a two-day emergency supply, which Urzua rationed to each one. They ate just two teaspoons of tuna and one biscuit every two days. They washed down their *meals* with a small sip of milk. It is amazing that after seventeen days, they still had some food left!

In addition to rationing their food supply, they fashioned a makeshift water canal by digging for groundwater and siphoning off additional water from the radiators of mine equipment.

The rescue teams drilled two small holes. This provided an umbilical-like cord through which supplies were sent. One of their first requests was for toothbrushes. Additional items were sent, like food, medical supplies, water, oxygen capsules, glucose and rehydration tablets that were meant to restore their digestive systems. They were supplied with communications devices and batteries to recharge and give power for their helmet lights. The device that transported small objects between the mine chamber and the surface was called a paloma, which in English means pigeon.

One of the miners, José Henríquez, was an evangelical Christian. As rescue efforts developed on the surface, he helped the men maintain a positive outlook during their confinement. He held daily Bible studies for the men. At their request, Bibles were also sent down to them. Since the Bibles had to be small enough to fit into the paloma, a magnifying glass was attached with each Bible. The miners held prayer services at noon and at 6:00 p.m.

Responding further to Henriquez's request for spiritual materials, they were sent an MP3 audio version of the New Testament in Spanish and an MP3 audio version of the *Jesus* film.[3]

The *Jesus* film is an evangelistic movie about the life of Jesus that has been translated into more than eleven hundred languages.[4] During their confinement the Lord had their undivided attention. Several of the miners became Christians.

Henriquez sent letters through the paloma, their lifeline. The letters thanked the rescue workers for all of the items sent to them and mentioned that the Christian materials were an especially tremendous blessing for him and his co-workers. He closed one of the letters with *"For the Lord is a great God and a great King above all gods, In whose hand are the depths of the earth; the peaks of the mountains are His also"* (Psalm 95:3-4).

When Esteban Rojas was rescued and reached the surface, he stepped out of the rescue device and immediately knelt on the ground with his hands together in prayer. Then he raised his arms above him in adoration. Carlos Mamani also knelt down as soon as he reached the surface and gave thanks to God. Omar Reygadas did the same, plus he held a Bible in his hands and wore a helmet with *God lives* written on it.

The miners credit God for keeping them free of dysentery and other diseases, which would usually be present in a group their size in such close quarters. *"For, it is He who delivers you from the snare of the trapper and from the deadly pestilence. He will cover you with His pinions, and under His wings you may seek refuge; His faithfulness is a shield and bulwark"* (Psalm 91:3-4).

The miners' testament of faith has had a broad resonance throughout the world.

TRUST HIM, GOD KNOWS BEST

This story was sent to me by my cousin, Joe Kersey.[1]

"In 1999 I was recruited to leave my job as a corporate controller (where I had been for four years) and hired as the CFO for a local company. In the summer of 2000 I lost my mom to cancer. In October of 2001 my dad also passed away. A few weeks after my dad died I was told by my new company that a family member was coming back to the family business, and there was no room for me anymore in the firm.

"My wife, Kristin, was five months pregnant with our second child, and the baby was due in March of 2002. Our daughter, Kate, was twenty-two months old.

"So in a short span of time I had lost both of my parents, I found myself unemployed, and we were expecting a baby.

"Two weeks after losing my job, Kristin woke me up one morning. She was bleeding and said something was wrong. It was December 10, 2001. Our son, Joseph, was born that same day, almost four months premature. At that moment I could not see how things could be any worse. The doctors gave Joseph a 50/50 chance of living, and he was immediately put on a respirator.

"As of this writing Joseph is ten years old and healthy, and I look back and think, 'Wow! God is so good!' Because I did not have a job, I was able to visit my son in the hospital every day and provide support for Kristin and our daughter, Kate. I was able to spend time in prayer and time reading all of the website mail we received for Joseph. The website had family, friends and strangers posting encouraging e-mails.

"In February, 2002, just before Joseph was released from the hospital, I took a chance and tried a new career in mortgage lending. Again God blessed me. As He closed one door, He opened another, and He was with me the entire time. I just praise God for His wisdom and timing. I could not imagine going to work for eight to ten hours a day while my son lay in the hospital hooked up to so many different machines. God truly does not test you beyond your means.

"Joseph has earned a first degree brown belt in karate. He takes karate at Savior Martial Arts, and as part of his testing was required to memorize and recite forty Bible verses. Oh, the joy to see how he loves the Lord and yet sad to admit that he can recite more verses than I can or anyone else in the family.

"I'm looking forward to seeing what God has planned for this special son who was only given a 50/50 chance!"

> *"For I know the plans that I have for you, declares the Lord, plans for welfare and not for calamity to give you a future and a hope"* (Jeremiah 29:11).

LOSS TURNS TO GAIN

This story was sent to me by Frank Dinovo.[1] Frank and I were close associates for some twenty years in a travel company we worked for in the Midwest. He sent me the following testimony:

"I firmly believe that God speaks to each and every one of us each day, and often through our children. One day I was having supper with my then six-year old boy. It was after a particularly frustrating day at the office, and I was not in a good mood.

"My boy picked up on my foul mood and asked me: 'Dad, do you ever think of taking your problems to Jesus?' How profound! As the Bible says ' . . . from the mouths of babes . . . ' (Matthew 21:16).

"Later one weekend I was working at the office on a proposal to retain our company's largest account. I was just getting started on the proposal, when I received a panic telephone call from a member of my church. Her mother had suffered a severe stroke and was not expected to live through the night. She wanted me and several other close friends to be by her mother's side in her hour of death.

"I wanted to say: 'No, I'm too busy working on this proposal, and, if I don't do a good job, the company will lose its largest account.' I tried listening to God speak in my conscience, and I felt as if He was urging me on to be with her. It was as if God was saying: 'Everything will be all right.'

"So, I put my trust in God and spent the weekend with the dying woman (Alice) and her daughter. Unfortunately, we lost the account and I was mad at God—I felt like I had put my trust in Him and he had let me down. I had no patience with God, whose patience is infinite. It was like God was saying be patient and listen to me.

"Exactly one year later Alice's daughter called me. She was reminiscing about the death of her mother on the first anniversary of her death. I felt like blaming the loss of the account on her, but I didn't.

"Immediately after Alice's daughter called, I received a call from a high-level executive of the largest account in town, several times the size of the account that was lost. He wanted to meet with me to make arrangements to transfer his business from our competitor to us. This was a surprise because we had given up soliciting the account, as we thought we did not have a chance of getting it.

"We worked out a brief contract, and we started servicing the account almost immediately. On the way back to the office I said a brief prayer of thanks to God and asked forgiveness for my lack of patience when He was speaking to me one year earlier.

"The addition of this account began what eventually became a tremendous success story for the company. I am glad I listened to that gentle prompting from God to be with Alice in her hour of death. Yes, indeed: *'Precious in the sight of the Lord is the death of His godly ones'* (Psalm 116:15)."

"Trust in the Lord with all your heart and do not lean on your own understanding. In all your ways acknowledge Him, and He will make your paths straight" (Proverbs 3:5-6).

ANSWERED PRAYER FINDS WIFE

The author shares this story:

I know that God was working in my life when He answered my prayers about getting married. For several years, while I was in high school, I prayed and asked God to provide three things when it was time for me to find the girl with whom I would spend my life.

> First, that I would know her when I saw her, love at first sight.
> Second, that I would get married when I was young.
> Third, that we would have kids while I was young enough to play with them.

Once I thought He had answered my prayer, because I met a girl and just *knew* she was the right person. But, she wasn't. She and I drifted apart.

During the spring of my sophomore year (1959) at Northwestern University, a group of the guys from my fraternity, Theta Chi, and I were walking back to our dorms after church. We passed by the Alpha Omicron Pi sorority house where Donna (the girl I would marry) was a member. I didn't know her. As far as I know, I had never seen her before.

Yet, to this day, more than fifty years later, I clearly remember seeing her *that* day. She was on the front porch of the sorority along with about a dozen other girls. She was in the back row on my right. My recollection is that we didn't even stop or say anything.

It wasn't until early the following December, as I was waiting to cross a street after taking a final exam and looking especially grungy, that I even saw Donna again. We made some small talk, got one another's names and went our ways. Donna remembers both scenarios also, and marvels we ever got together!

Even though it wasn't exactly love at first sight, I remembered Donna. We were married two months after graduation in August, 1961. Our family of two children was complete by the time I was twenty-seven. So, all three of my prayer requests were answered. After fifty years of marriage, I still know for sure that God answers prayer.

> "So I say to you, ask, and it will be given to you; seek, and you will find; knock, and it will be opened to you" (Luke 11:9).

Silent Witness of the Ground Zero Cross

The Ground Zero Cross was discovered by construction worker Frank Silecchia. He came across it in the rubble of the World Trade Center just a few days after September 11, 2001. It stood straight, twenty-feet high, surrounded by a number of smaller crosses. It was not simply cross beams that remained from an existing building. It was formed out of beams from Building One that had plunged, split and crashed into Building Six! The cross weighed a couple of tons.

Frank worked with the search-and-rescue teams at Ground Zero. On September 13, blanketed with dirt and dust and near exhaustion, he came upon the area where the atrium of the World Trade Center had been. There he found the twenty-foot cross standing above several smaller crosses in a grotto-like setting. He felt a strange peace in the stillness of the area around the cross. Frank recalls, "I could almost hear God saying, 'The terrible thing done at this site was meant for evil. But I will turn it to good. Have *faith*, I am here.'"[1] Frank and other workers sprayed orange Xs to show where they had already been in the wreckage. He sprayed the words "God's House" on the ruins surrounding the cross.

Day after day Frank worked digging through the ruins. It was extremely difficult and exhausting labor. When he thought he couldn't go on with his work, he would go to "God's House" and the steel-beam cross, where he would find renewed strength and comfort for his spirit.

Firemen, policemen, grieving survivors, dignitaries, clergymen, fellow workers and others found the same healing effect from the cross. Frank's friend, Father Brian Jordan, was a priest from

St. Francis of Assisi in New York, and he became the chaplain at Ground Zero. When it was time to remove the wreckage surrounding the cross, Father Jordan convinced officials that the cross should be saved.

When the cross was first removed from the area, ironworkers affixed it to a concrete base. It was then raised and mounted onto a forty-foot foundation that had once been a walkway for pedestrians at the World Trade Center. It was visible to rescue workers who were working below it in the cratered pit. It became a symbol of faith and hope.

The cross was later transported four blocks away from Ground Zero. For weeks many people came to that site to hold Sunday services. Scribbled on the cross were the names of the fallen police officers and firefighters, as well as the message "God Bless our Fallen Brothers".

On October 5, 2006, it was moved to St. Peter's Church, the city's oldest Catholic parish. A plaque there read "The Cross at Ground Zero—Found September 13, 2001; blessed October 4, 2001; Temporarily relocated October 15, 2006. Will return to WTC Museum, a sign of comfort for all"[2]

A short ceremony was held on July 23, 2011, at St. Peter's Church. The cross was then moved on a flatbed truck to Ground Zero and placed at the National September 11th Memorial and Museum.[3] Because of its size and weight the cross had to be moved and in place before the rest of the Memorial and Museum could be completed.

The cross has been and continues to be a tremendous comfort to many and shows how God is present in all circumstances.

As It Was in the Days of Noah . . .

Jesus said in Matthew 24:37, *"For the coming of the Son of Man will be just like the days of Noah."* And in Luke 17:26 He said, *"And just as it happened in the days of Noah, so it will be also in the days of the Son of Man".*

In Noah's day no one listened to Noah and his warnings about a coming flood. Most thought he was crazy, and even more so as he began to build the ark. In that day there was much godlessness and corruption on the earth. In Genesis 6:11-12 it states: *"Now the earth was corrupt in the sight of God, and the earth was filled with violence. God looked on the earth, and behold, it was corrupt; for all flesh had corrupted their way upon the earth."*

People were going about their daily lives with little or no concern about any warnings from God and His displeasure with their actions. It was business as usual with complete disregard for deteriorating morals and virtues.

The earth has become decadent and immoral and with problems just like in the time of Noah. Today many people go about their daily activities, not heeding any signs of the Second Coming or the urgency and pleas to change their ways and come to Christ.

Many signs of the End Times seem to be coming true in our lifetime. Yet, many people are willing to believe false prophets and ignore the biblical prophecies that were made about the final showdown between good and evil.

In the past there has been interest in the Ark built by Noah, mainly in attempts to find where it landed after the flood. There has not been much interest in building or creating replicas of

Noah's Ark . . . UNTIL today. Following is information on three such construction projects that have been in the news.

REPLICA OF THE ARK BUILT IN HONG KONG

Hong Kong is the site of the first actual size replica of the ark and was opened to the public in July of 2011[1]. Construction began in 2004. It was built per the dimensions of the Ark in the Book of Genesis: 300 cubits long (approximately 450 feet), 50 cubits wide (approximately 75 feet), and 30 cubits high (approximately 45 feet). In the planning stage for seventeen years, the project was mainly funded by an evangelical Christian, billionaire Thomas Kwok and his two brothers.

The ark is part of a Christian theme park and is strategically located on Ma Wan Island. The idea of the ark was conceived by a young girl. According to the manager of the theme park, Mathew Pine, "She drew a little picture and her dad took it to the government. The government officials loved it and from there on the architects and the engineers developed the plan".[2]

The Ark contains exhibits of rare animals and shows animated films that depict how the original ark could have been built and how it might have been ventilated. Also featured is a garden with seventy pairs of real-size replicas of animals.

REPLICA OF THE ARK IN KENTUCKY

There is a similar project underway to build a life-sized Noah's Ark on eight hundred acres in Williamsburg, Kentucky, near Interstate 75.[3] Construction is scheduled to begin in early 2012, as fund-raising is still on-going.

The Christian ministry organization, *Answers in Genesis*, is the driving force behind the project. They want to show the world that the story of the flood found in the Book of Genesis is not a fable, but an historical truth. Plans are for the project to be authentic inside and out. According to project manager, Mike Zovath, "The message here is, God's word is true."[4]

The $24.5 million religious theme park will be called the Ark Encounter, and the ark will be its main attraction. Plans for the actual building of the ark are to be done by a team of Amish builders from Indiana. The structure will measure approximately 500 feet across, 75 feet wide and 45 feet high, and is modeled after the measurements in the Bible. As reported in the New York Times, "The theme park will also include a one hundred foot Tower of Babel, a first-century Middle Eastern village and a journey through the Old Testament, with special effects depicting Moses, the ten plagues, and the parting of the Red Sea."[5]

The park will have a petting zoo for children, along with live bird and animal shows. A play area for kids will include zip-lines and climbing nets—all Bible-themed. As trainer Dan Breeding presents the animal acts, he will include a Gospel message and relate the Bible story of creation.

REPLICA OF THE ARK BUILT IN THE NETHERLANDS

Sixty year old Johan Huibers of the Netherlands has completed a replica of Noah's Ark that has the same measurements as the Ark in the Book of Genesis, and it is SEAWORTHY!

In 1992 Huibers had a dream that convinced him he should build an ark. He had no specific plans or drawings, just the will to build it. "I asked God every day, 'Give me the ideas—how to do it.' And God gave them to me day by day, so it was very easy," he says.[6]

This huge replica is the length of one and a half football fields and is as tall as a five-story building. It weighs 2,970 tons and is built with Swedish pine, to follow God's command to Noah to build the Ark of resin (gopher) wood. The project took more than three years to complete and was built by Huibers, two of his children, and some friends. Huibers himself has invested more than $1.6 million in the project.

The ark is stocked with replicated pairs of animals to depict those that were aboard the original ark. They were designed and created in the Philippines. They are put in containers, along with a few live animals. Huibers reportedly paid $11,000 for one reproduction of an elephant! There are plans also for a live aviary, where birds can fly in and out from the top of the ark.

When asked why he wanted to complete this project, Huibers explained that he is concerned that people today don't know who God is. They may have a Bible in the home, but it is just there, not being read. He hopes his project will encourage people to start caring about God again and return to reading the Bible. He believes that God has all the answers that are needed today.[7]

Huibers hopes to send his full-size replica to the 2012 London Olympics. He has petitioned London Mayor Boris Johnson for permission to dock it on the Thames River during the games for visitors to see.[8]

Could God be reminding us of what Jesus said in Matthew 24:37 and Luke 17:26?

The End

The stories you have read illustrate how God is still performing MIRACLES, fulfilling PROPHECY and working in OTHER WAYS in today's world.

The events in these stories happened in many different countries around the world. They happened to both men and women of various ages. They happened to ordinary people and to the well known. They happened to the free and to those in prison. They even happened to murderers, those addicted to drugs and others who may have committed unspeakable evil.

Each of these people had their lives changed and their faith strengthened through the events they experienced. Some events happened instantly and others happened over time. God has shown He changes lives by performing miracles, fulfilling prophecy and revealing Himself in other ways.

You have read stories that show how God has and will continue to fulfill prophecies that are thousands of years old. For example, the prophecies in Isaiah 43:5-6 and Zechariah 8:7-8 were fulfilled when the country of Israel was declared a new sovereign state in 1948. During these past few decades God has continued to fulfill the prophecy recorded in Daniel 12:4, which states there will be an increase in travel and knowledge in the latter days. Other stories tell about how He is working to increase the proclaiming of His Word and Gospel message around the world.

God gives us more and more insight as He steadily reveals His plans for the world. As time moves closer to Jesus Christ's return, the predictions of future events made in both the Old and New Testaments are coming true today with ever-increasing momentum. In Matthew 24:4-14 Jesus said that the fulfillment of prophesied events, like the progression of birth pangs as a woman advances through labor, will increase in frequency and intensity, until the End is suddenly here. Are you ready?

Even though we can't see God, we can experience His creation through all five of our senses. We can:

> **see** creation's beauty that surrounds us.
>
> **hear** birds chirp their music.
>
> **feel** a soft breeze.
>
> **smell** the perfumed fragrance of a flower.
>
> **taste** the sweetness of a garden peach.

The Bible declares that God has made everything that exists.

> *"For by Him all things were created, both in the heavens and on earth, visible and invisible ... all things have been created through Him and for Him"* (Colossians 1:16).

> *"For since the creation of the world His invisible attributes, His eternal power and divine nature, have been clearly seen, being understood through what has been made, so that they are without excuse"* (Romans 1:20).

> *"The heavens are telling of the glory of God; and their expanse is declaring the work of His hands"* (Psalms 19:1).

> *"Now faith is the assurance of things hoped for, the conviction of things not seen"* (Hebrews 11:1).

And, just so we won't miss it, we are told a fifth time:

> *"while we look not at the things which are seen, but at the things which are not seen; for the things which are seen are temporal, but the things which are not seen are eternal"* (2 Corinthians 4:18).

Since we can see and experience all of God's glory and creation in nature, and the Bible clearly states that we are given these signs to help us believe:

There is no excuse for not believing in God!

We are all unique. No two finger prints, voice prints or DNAs are exactly alike. God loves each of us and treats each one of us individually. In return we must also respond to Him as individuals. No one else can respond for you.

Jesus gives us only two options. There is no third choice. One can accept Him for whom He said He was—the Son of God and the Savior of the world—or, deny Him. John 14:6 states: *"I am the way, and the truth, and the life; no one comes to the Father but through Me* (Jesus).*"* Anyone who denies God cannot enter heaven to reside with Him in eternity.

Pretend you are a high jumper at a track meet and the world record is slightly over eight feet. Imagine that God's standard is a bar set at fifty feet. It is impossible for you to jump over the bar. Yet, *"with God all things are possible"* (Matthew 19:26). Anyone trying to jump over the fifty foot bar without God's help has no hope of clearing it.

No one can *jump high enough* or be *good enough* to earn eternal life. Eternal life is not earned. It is a gift, freely given! When you believe Jesus is God's Son, who died in your place to pay for your sins, who conquered death, and who rose from the dead, salvation is yours! Yet, many refuse to accept this free gift.

All a person needs to do to receive God's free gift of eternal life is to do three things:

1. Believe that Jesus is the Son of God.
2. Believe that all our sins (past, present and future no matter how ugly or horrible they may be) were paid for in full when Jesus died on the cross.
3. Believe that Jesus was resurrected from the dead and will return as He promised.

Once a person takes these three steps and becomes a believer in Jesus, he or she will want to follow His commandments.

Some believe that when one dies, death is the end. They are wrong! The Bible states: *"it is appointed for men to die once and after this comes judgment"* (Hebrews 9:27). Death is just a beginning—either a person will have an eternal life of joy with God, or an eternity of agony and torment in Hell.

No one knows if they will be alive tomorrow. They may have a sudden heart attack or be killed in a car crash. That is why it is so urgent that a person believe in Jesus and take the three steps listed above. The Apostle John states in John 3:18: *"He who believes in Him is not judged; he who does not believe has been judged already, because he has not believed in the name of the only begotten Son of God."*

My wife and I attended a presentation by Josh McDowell on February 23, 2011, at Chase Oaks Church in Plano, Texas. Josh told me that "no one can argue a person into heaven. They can just paint the facts." Painting the facts is what I have tried to do in this book.

Josh also said: "A lot of people say, 'well how can a loving God send anyone to hell?' First of all, God doesn't send anyone to hell. If we go to hell, it's by our own choice. But, when somebody says to me, 'How can a loving God allow anyone to go to hell?' I'll turn around and ask, 'Well, how can a holy, just, righteous God allow sin into His presence?'"[1]

If you want the free gift of eternal life, acknowledge your faith in Jesus as your Savior. Please, don't delay! I beg of you to pray the following prayer:

> Thank You, God, for loving me as an individual. I believe that Jesus is Your Son. I confess that I have sinned and not been righteous or obedient to Your commandments. I believe that Your Son, Jesus Christ, died on the cross and paid in full the penalty for my own sins—past, present and future. I believe that You raised Jesus from the dead and that you will do the same for me. I now confess that Jesus is Lord and put my faith in Him alone. Thank you for your gift of eternal life. I pray this in Jesus' name. Amen.

NOTES

MIRACLES
1. C.S. Lewis, *Miracles* (New York: HarperOne, 2001).

IMPRISONED MAN PREACHES IN IRANIAN COURT
1. Rob Hall, "Daniel Baumann: Imprisoned in Iran" 700 Club, 15 February 2011, http://www.cbn.com/700club/features/amazing/RH41_daniel_baumann.aspx (accessed 14 December 2011).
2. Ibid.

CRUSHED BY TRUCK—ANGELS TO THE RESCUE
1. Audra Hall, "Bruce Van Natta: Saved by Angels" 700 Club, 29 November 2010, http://www.cbn.com/700club/features/amazing/Bruce-van-Natta-112410.aspx (accessed 2 May 2011).
2. Ibid.
3. Ibid.
4. Ibid.
5. Ibid.

GOD MADE HER INVISIBLE TO PRISON GUARDS
1. Corrie ten Boom, *A Prisoner and Yet...* (Fort Washington, PA: CLS Publications 1954), 99-100.
2. Ibid., 100.

GOD WAS THE DRIVER
1. Christopher, Bob. "Re: Larry's Miracle." Message to Kenneth R. Kersey. 29 October 2010. E-mail.

SHE SAW HEAVEN AND HELL
1. Tamara Laroux, *Delivered* (Maitland, FL: Xulon Press, 2006).
2. Robert Hull, "Tamara Laroux: Surviving a Suicide Attempt" 700 Club, 28 September 2010, http://www.cbn.com/700club/features/amazing/Tamara-Laroux-092810.aspx (accessed 12 May 2011).
3. Ibid.
4. Ibid.
5. Ibid.
6. Ibid.

THE MAN WHO COULD NOT BE SHOT
1. David Barton, *The Bulletproof George Washington* (Aledo, TX: Wallbuilders, 1990), 5.
2. Ibid., 59.
3. Ibid., 63.
4. Ibid., 67.

DEAD MAN LIVES TO PREACH
1. Don Piper, *90 Minutes in Heaven* (Grand Rapids, MI: Revella, division of Baker Publishing Group, 2004).
2. Ibid., 43.
3. Ibid., 44.

MISSIONARIES PROTECTED IN THE SOUTH PACIFIC
1. Billy Graham, *Angels*. (Dallas, TX: Word Publishing, 1975), 5.
2. Ibid, 6.

PROPHECY

1. Josh McDowell, *More Than a Carpenter* (Wheaton, IL: Living Books, Tyndale House Publishers, Inc., 1977), 102-103.
2. Josh McDowell, *The New Evidence That Demands a Verdict* (Nashville, TN: Thomas Nelson, 1999), 168-192.

INCREASE IN TRAVEL AND KNOWLEDGE

COMMUNION ON THE MOON

1. Dr. David R. Williams, *The Apollo 8 Christmas Eve Broadcast*, NASA, 25 September 2007, http://nssdc.gsfc.nasa.gov/planetary/lunar/apollo8_xmas.html (accessed 14 December 2011).

EARTH WITHOUT OCEANS

1. Mark Anderson, "PICTURES: "Drained" Oceans Reveal Epic Landscapes" National Geographic, 28 Oct 2010, http://news.nationalgeographic.com/news/2009/08/photogalleries/drain-the-ocean-pictures/ (accessed 03 May 2011).

VERTICAL FARMING—NEW WAY TO FEED THE WORLD

1. Joseph Taylor, "How Many People Are There in the World?—World Population Crisis Gets Closer" JamesJoe.com, 15 October 2011, http://jamesjoe.com/joe-taylor/articles/how-many-people-are-there-in-the-world.asp (accessed 02 November 2011).
2. Wikipedia, "Aeroponics" Wikipedia, September, 2011, http://en.wikipedia.org/wiki/Aeroponics(accessed 02 November 2011).
3. Witneyo, "Vertical Farming, the Pros and Cons", The VertBlog, 15 September 2010, http://verticalharvest.wordpress.com/2010/09/15/vertical-farming-the-pros-and-cons/ (accessed 02 November 2011).

GOSPEL TRANSLATED FOR THE WORLD

1. M. Paul Lewis, "Ethnologue: Languages of the World, Sixteenth edition", SIL International, 2009, http://www.ethnologue.com (accessed 19 November 2011).
2. "Bible Facts", Biblica, 2002, http://www.biblica.com/bibles/faq/19/ (accessed 19 November 2011).
3. UNESCO, "Endangered languages", United Nations Educational, Scientific and Cultural Organization, 2011, http://www.unesco.org/new/en/culture/themes/cultural-diversity/languages-and-multilingualism/endangered-languages/ (accessed 19 November 2011).

TWEETING FOR GOD

1. Neda Semnani, "Shimkus Tweets Serve a Higher Purpose", Roll Call Staff, 6 June 2011, http://www.rollcall.com/issues/56_133/Shimkus-Tweets-Serve-a-Higher-Purpose-206176-1.html (accessed 7 June 2011).
2. Ibid.

FINDING OIL AND GAS IN ISRAEL

1. S. Spillman, "Oil Discovered in Northern Israel", 31 January 2011, http://www.oilinisrael.net/top-stories/oil-northern-israel (accessed 22 October 2011).
2. "Asher" *AboutBibleProphecy.com*, http://www.aboutbibleprophecy.com/p120.htm (accessed 5 July 2011).
3. "Exploration History", *Zion Oil and Gas*, http://www.zionoil.com/exploration-history (accessed 22 October 2011).
4. "Petroleum Law", *Zion Oil and Gas*, http://www.zionoil.com/petroleum-law (accessed 19 November 2011).

5. Tal Barak Harif and Susan Lerner, "Israel Sees Energy Independence in Natural Gas Offshore Fields", *Bloomberg*, 04 March, 2009, http://www.bloomberg.com/apps/news?pid=newsarchive&sid=aUNIIFwH22dU (accessed 23 October 2011).
6. "Exploration History", *Zion Oil and Gas*, http://www.zionoil.com/exploration-history (accessed 22 October 2011).
7. "Givot Olam", *Givot Olam Oil Ltd.*, http://www.givot.co.il/english/index.php (acccessed 23 October 2011).
8. "Liquefied Natural Gas", *Wikipedia*, http://en.wikipedia.org/wiki/Liquefied_natural_gas (accessed 23 October 2011).
9. Babak Dehghanpisheh, "Israel's Leviathan at Sea", *The Daily Beast*, 17 January 2011, http://www.thedailybeast.com/newsweek/2011/01/18/israel-s-leviathan-at-sea.html (accessed 23 October 2011).
10. Ibid.
11. Hank Pellissier, "Israel's Natural Gas Discovery: Five Possible Scenarios", *World Future Society*, 11 October, 2011, http://www.wfs.org/content/israels-natural-gas-discovery-five-possible-scenarios (accessed 23 October 2011).
12. Piers Morgan, "Piers Morgan and Israeli Prime Minister Benjamin Netanyahu—Full Transcript", *CNN Piers Morgan Tonight*, 18 March 2011, http://piersmorgan.blogs.cnn.com/2011/03/17/israel-prime-minister-netanyahu-japan-situation-has-caused-me-to-reconsider-nuclear-power/ (accessed 10 October 2011).
13. Lawrence Solomon, "Israel's new energy" *Financial Post*, 10 June 2011, http://mideastenvironment.apps01.yorku.ca/?p=2664 (accessed 19 November 2011).
14. Noy Dor and Menachem Danishefsky, "A legal vacuum filling up with gas: Israel's new regulatory environment", *Offshore*, March, 2011, http://www.offshore-mag.com/index/article-display.articles.

offshore.volume-71.issue-9.eastern-mediterranean.a-legal-vacuum-filling-up-withgas.QP129867.dcmp=rss.page=1.html (accessed 19 November 2011).

PAPYRUS TO PIXELS

1. Chris Mitchell, "The Mystery of the Copper Scroll", *Christian World News*, 27 September 2009, http://www.cbn.com/cbnnews/347306.aspx (accessed 4 October 2011).
2. Ibid.
3. CenturyOne Bookstore, "25 Fascinating Facts About the Discovery at Qumran", *CenturyOne Bookstore*, 1996, http://www.centuryone.com/25dssfacts.html (accessed 4 October 2011).
4. "Israel Museum, Jerusalem", *Sacred Destinations*, 2010, http://www.sacred-destinations.com/israel/jerusalem-israel-museum.htm (Accessed 04 October 2011).
5. CenturyOne Bookstore, "25 Fascinating Facts About the Discovery at Qumran", *CenturyOne Bookstore*, 1996, http://www.centuryone.com/25dssfacts.html (accessed 4 October 2011).
6. "Israel Museum, Google put Dead Seas Scrolls Online", *The Independent*, 27 September 2011, http://www.independent.co.uk/arts-entertainment/art/israel-museum-google-put-dead-sea-scrolls-online-2361578.html (accessed 24 October, 2011).
7. Chris Mitchell, "The Mystery of the Copper Scroll", *Christian World News*, 27 September 2009, http://www.cbn.com/cbnnews/347306.aspx (accessed 4 October 2011)
8. Ibid.
9. CenturyOne Bookstore, "25 Fascinating Facts About the Discovery at Qumran", *CenturyOne Bookstore*, 1996, http://www.centuryone.com/25dssfacts.html (accessed 4 October 2011).
10. Ibid.

11. Andrew Lawler, "Who Wrote the Dead Sea Scrolls", *Smithsonian Magazine*, January 2010, http://www.smithsonianmag.com/history-archaeology/Who-Wrote-the-Dead-Sea-Scrolls.html (accessed 24 October 2011).
12. Ibid.
13. "Israel Museum, Jerusalem", *Sacred Destinations*, 2010, http://www.sacred-destinations.com/israel/jerusalem-israel-museum.htm (accessed 04 October 2011).
14. "Israel Museum, Google put Dead Seas Scrolls Online", *The Independent*, 27 September 2011. http://www.independent.co.uk/arts-entertainment/art/israel-museum-google-put-dead-sea-scrolls-online-2361578.html (accessed 24 October, 2011).
15. CenturyOne Bookstore, "25 Fascinating Facts About the Discovery at Qumran", *CenturyOne Bookstore*, 1996, http://www.centuryone.com/25dssfacts.html (accessed 4 October 2011).
16. "Dead Sea Scrolls Exhibit Coming Alive", *The Christianity*, 23 April 2010, http://thechristianity.wordpress.com/2010/04/23/dead-sea-scrolls-exhibit-coming-alive/ (accessed 20 November 2011).
17. "Israel Museum, Google put Dead Seas Scrolls Online", *The Independent*, 27 September 2011, http://www.independent.co.uk/arts-entertainment/art/israel-museum-google-put-dead-sea—scrolls-online-2361578.html (accessed 24 October, 2011).
18. Duncan Macpherson and Rob Waugh, "Scroll over this: Dead Sea Scrolls now online—and your mouse pointer Instantly translates into English", *Mail Online*, 27 September 2011, http://www.dailymail.co.uk/sciencetech/article-2042048/Dead-Sea-Scrolls-online—mouse-pointer-instantly-translates-English.html (accessed 29 September 2011).
19. Ibid.

REACHING NATIONS WITH THE GOSPEL

THE GOSPEL MADE KNOWN BY BIBLES
1. The Gideons International, "About Us: Our History", *The Gideons International*, 2011, http://www.gideons.org/AboutUs/OurHistory.aspx (accessed 12 May 2011).

BIBLES FALL FROM THE SKY!
1. The Gideons International, "Miracle from a Helicopter", *The Gideons International*, 2011, http://www.gideons.org/ChangedLives/ChangedLivesText.aspx?source={0F286337-65CF-4073-8EBA-45B72C6F3F08} (accessed 11 October 2011).

MEETING GOD UNDER THE OCEAN
1. The Gideons International, "I Found Things I Never Knew Before", *The Gideons International*, 2011, http://www.gideons.org/ChangedLives/ChangedLivesText.aspx?source={35061FD1-7CF6-4A06-B0CB-C1BAAB220344} (accessed 25 October 2011).

A GRANDMOTHER'S LAST WORDS—DON'T WAIT
1. The Gideons International, "A Christmas Regret That Led to a Decision for Christ", *The Gideons International*, 2011, http://www.gideons.org/ChangedLives/ChangedLivesText.aspx?source={9FE218B9-1B11-4363-8F1A-31FB0A36FFA1} (accessed 25 October 2011).

FROM DEEP DESPAIR TO THE MOUNTAINTOP
1. The Gideons International, *Gideon Testimonies from the U.S.A.*, (Nashville, TN: The Gideons International, 2005), 34-36.

DEVIL WORSHIPER BECOMES A CHRISTIAN

1. The Gideons International, *"Convention Testimonies Isaiah 55:11 Fulfilled",* (Nashville, TN: The Gideons International, 2005), 39-41.

DAD WAS SAVED JUST IN TIME

1. The Gideons International, "A Father's Salvation, remembered on Father's Day", *The Gideons International,* 2011, http://www.gideons.org/ChangedLives/ChangedLivesText.aspx?source={ED132BB3-C504-4EA0-A8D9-9B2FB4FA5B7D} (accessed 25 October 2011).

HOSPITAL BIBLE COMFORTS AND SAVES TWO

1. The Gideons International, "I Found Comfort, Faith and Salvation in God's Word", *The Gideons International* 2011, http://www.gideons.org/ChangedLives/ChangedLivesText.aspx?source={6118D224-5331-411E-9D43-B37CF4A97717} (accessed 25 October 2011).

LEGACY OF A GRANDMOTHER'S BIBLE

1. Al Childers, *Gideon Testimonies from the U.S.A.,* (Nashville, TN: The Gideons International, 2005), 56-57.

GOD CHANGES TAXI DRIVER'S PLANS

1. The Gideons International, "A Change of Plans in the Philippines", *The Gideons International,* 2011, http://www.gideons.org/ChangedLives/ChangedLivesText.aspx?source={EA97442B-6135-4EC0-BDA4-A381D938F981} (accessed 20 November 2011).

ONE BIBLE SAVES FORTY

1. The Gideons International, "A Colombian Drug Lab", *The Gideons International,* 2011, http://www.gideons.org/ChangedLives/

ChangedLivesText.aspx?source={F9D1A094-36B2-4C86-A1DB-D5B64B7FC56C} (accessed 25 October 2011).

A PISTOL OR A GIDEON BIBLE?

1. The Gideons International, "Choosing Between a Pistol and a Gideon Bible", *The Gideons International*, 2011, http://www.gideons.org/ChangedLives/ChangedLivesText.aspx?source={84EC67CD-541E-4788-BBA3-436AAA92CE07} (accessed 25 October 2011).

HE STOLE A BIBLE INSTEAD OF MONEY

1. The Gideons International, "A Stolen Opportunity", *The Gideons International*, 2011, http://www.gideons.org/ChangedLives/ChangedLivesText.aspx?source={AFF22AD7-8899-438D-B334-16725C4C37B4} (accessed 25 October 2011).

THE BOOK IS TO READ, NOT TO SMOKE

1. The Gideons International, "The Book is to Read, Not to Smoke", *The Gideons International*, 2011, http://www.gideons.org/ChangedLives/ChangedLivesText.aspx?source={F41903E6-42A5-B036-495F6E0CF353 (accessed 25 October 2011).

I THOUGHT I WAS A CHRISTIAN

1. Phyllis Taylor, *Gideon Testimonies from the U.S.A.*, (Nashville, TN: The Gideons International, 2005), 18-20.

MUSLIM HOTELS FINALLY WELCOME BIBLES

1. Josue Gayares, *Gideon Testimonies From Around the World*, (Nashville, TN: The Gideons International 2004), 86.

NO ONE IS EVER TOO BAD FOR GOD'S LOVE
1. Ronnie Cummings, "Miraculously Transformed", T*he Gideon,* December, 2007, 17-19.

THE GOSPEL PROCLAIMED BY THOSE "CALLED TO SERVE"

A SOLDIER FOR CHRIST
1. Catherine Marshall, *A Man Called Peter,* (New York: London: Toronto: McGraw-Hill, 1951), 133.

SCIENCE AND FAITH ARE ALLIES
1. Hugh Ross, "Our Mission", *Reasons to Believe,* 2011, http://www.reasons.org/about-us/our-purpose (accessed 1 November 2011).
2. Michelle Young, "Request to Use Biography of Dr. Hugh Ross in book". Message to Kenneth R. Kersey. 06 February 2012. E-mail.
3. Ibid.

GOD EMPOWERS THOSE HE CALLS
1. Ralph Ehren, "Journey". Message to Kenneth R. Kersey. 10 April 2010. E-mail.

HAND GRENADE EXPLODES, LEADS TO A MINISTRY
1. Dave Roever, "The Dave Roever Story", *Roever & Associates,* 2007-2011. http://daveroever.org/roeverstory.php (accessed 1 November 2011).
2. "Eagles Summit Ranch", *Roever & Associates,* 2007-2011. http://daveroever.org/esr/index.php (accessed 1 November 2011).
3. Ibid.
4. Dave Roever Evangelistic Association, "Billy Graham Comments", *Roever & Associates,* 2007-2011, http://daveroever.org/downloads/

Ministries/Billy_Graham_Comments.pdf (accessed 1 November 2011).

PROPHET OF PROPHECY
1. "Meet Hal Lindsey", *Christianbook.com*, 2011, http://www.christianbook.com/html/authors/1021.html (accessed 1 November 2011).
2. Ibid.
3. Nicole Balnius, "The Who's Who of Prophecy", *Rapture Ready*, 2010, http://www.raptureready.com/who/Hal_Lindsey.html (accessed 20 November 2011).
4. "Hal Lindsey", *Library Thing*, 2011, http://www.librarything.com/author/lindseyhal (accessed 1 November 2011).

HE PROVED JESUS IS TRUE
1. Josh McDowell, "Josh McDowell Testimony", *Josh.org*, 2011, http://www.josh.org/site/c.ddKDIMNtEqG/b.4700893/k.7B09/Josh_McDowell_Testimony_Transcripts.htm (accessed 1 November 2011).
2. Josh McDowell, "Josh McDowell", *Amazon.com*, 2011, http://www.amazon.com/Josh-McDowell/e/B000APEQR8 (accessed 1 November 2011).
3. Josh McDowell, "Evidence of a Changed Life, *Precious Testimonies*, 1998-2009, http://www.precious-testimonies.com/Hope_Encouragement/k-o/McDowellJ.htm (accessed 1 November 2011).
4. Ibid.
5. Ibid.
6. Josh McDowell, "Josh McDowell", *Amazon.com*, 2011, http://www.amazon.com/Josh-McDowell/e/B000APEQR8 (accessed 1 November 2011).
7. Ibid.

8. Eric Young, "Apologists Josh McDowell and Son Equip Youth Ministers for Easter", *Christianpost*, 20 February 2009, http://www.christianpost.com/news/apologists-josh-mcdowell-and-son-equip-youth-ministers-for-easter-37028/ (accessed 11 October 2011).

MISSIONARIES SLAIN, WIVES CONTINUE MINISTRY

1. Gracia Burnham, "Gracia's Corner", *The Martin and Gracia Burnham Foundation*, 2011, http://www.graciaburnham.org/ (accessed 2 November 2011).
2. "Elisabeth Elliot", *Wikipedia*, 2011, http://wikipedia.org/wiki/Elisabeth_Elliot (accessed 3 November 2011).
3. Wheaton College, "Jim Elliot Quote", *Wheaton College*, 2011, http://www2.wheaton.edu/bgc/archives/faq/20.htm (accessed 2 November 2011).
4. "Elisabeth Elliot", *Wikipedia*, 2011, http://wikipedia.org/wiki/Elisabeth_Elliot (accessed 3 November 2011).

MY WAY WAS NOT GOD'S WAY

1. "Research Supervisors", *London School of Theology*, 2011, http://www.lst.ac.uk/phd/research-supervisors (accessed 24 November 2011).

SERVANT OF GOD IN THE MAKING

1. "Campus Sports Ministry", *Athletes in Action on Campus University and Colleges around the US*, 2009, http://www.athletesinaction.org/campus/ (accessed 24 November 2011).
2. "Lead Me, Guide Me", *Jumbo Jimbo's Song Lyrics Archive*, 2004-2006, http://www.jumbojimbo.com/lyrics.php?songid=1857&type=chords (accessed 24 November 2011).

SHIP MINISTRY TEACHES, PREACHES AND SAVES

1. "George Verwer: Mobilizing to Spread the Gospel", *CBN*.com, The 700 Club, 2011, http://www.cbn.com/700club/guests/bios/George_Verwer033011.aspx (accessed 18 November 2011).
2. "How We Operate", *OM Ships International*, 2011, http://www.omships.org/index.php?option=com_content&view=article&id=55&Itemid=127&lang=en (accessed 18 November 2011).
3. "Country Profile: Ships:, OM Ships International, 2011, http://www.om.org/en/country-profile/ships (accessed 23 May 2011).
4. "How We Operate", *OM Ships International*, 2011, http://www.omships.org/index.php?option=com_content&view=article&id=55&Itemid=127&lang=en (accessed 18 November 2011).

TRANSLATOR OF THE BIBLE FOR MILLIONS

1. "About Us", *Wycliffe*, 2011, http://www.wycliffe.org/About.aspx?printerfriendly=yes (accessed 12 May 2011).
2. "William Cameron Townsend", *Wycliffe*, 2011, http://www.wycliffe.org/About/OurHistory/CameronTownsend.aspx (accessed 23 November 2011).
3. Ibid.
4. "About Us", *Wycliffe*, 2011, http://www.wycliffe.org/About.aspx?printerfriendly=yes (accessed 12 May 2011).
5. "The Worldwide Status of Bible Translation (2010)". *Wycliffe*, 2011, http://www.wycliffe.org/About/Statistics.aspx (accessed 23 November 2011).

GOD WANTED HIM TO BE A POLICEMAN

1. Bob Vernon. "God's Direction in My Life 1". Interview by John Fuller. *Focus on the Family*. KCBI Radio 90.9, Dallas. 05 August 2010. Radio.

2. Bob Vernon. "God's Direction in My Life 2". Interview by John Fuller. *Focus on the Family.* KCBI Radio 90.9, Dallas. 06 August 2010. Radio.
3. "Bob Vernon", *Law Officer.com,* 2011, http://www.lawofficer.com/authors/bob-vernon (accessed 24 November 2011).
4. "Bob Vernon", *Hume Lake Christian Camps,* 2011, http://www.humelake.org/talent/Speaker/bob-vernon (accessed 26 May 2011).

REACHING THE UNREACHABLE

1. "International Office", *ACTS International,* 2011, http://www.actsinternational.net/intloffice.shtml (accessed 3 May 2011).
2. "About ACTS International", *ACTS International,* 2011, http://www.actsinternational.net/about.shtml (accessed 19 May 2011).
3. "Welcome", *ACTS International,* 2011, http://www.actsinternational.net/index.shtml (accessed 23 November 2011).

GOD'S WORD CANNOT BE FROZEN

1. George Thomas, "Unfrozen: Gospel Reaches the 'End of the World'", *CBN News,* 27 February 2011, http://www.cbn.com/cbnnews/world/2011/February/Unfrozen-Gospel-Reaches-the-End-of-the-World/ (accessed 23 November 2011).

TRAGEDY LEADS TO LIFE MISSION

1. Wikipedia, "Joni Eareckson Tada", *Wikipedia,* 28 October 2011, http://en.wikipedia.org/wiki/Joni_Eareckson_Tada (accessed 3 Nov 2011).
2. Ibid.
3. National Day of Prayer Task Force, "Joni Eareckson Tada", *National Day of Prayer Task Force,* 2011, http://nationaldayofprayer.org/news/joni-eareckson-tada/ (accessed 4 November 2011).

4. Wikipedia, "Joni Eareckson Tada", *Wikipedia,* 28 October 2011, http://en.wikipedia.org/wiki/Joni_Eareckson_Tada (accessed 3 Nov 2011).
5. National Day of Prayer Task Force, "Joni Eareckson Tada", *National Day of Prayer Task Force,* 2011, http://nationaldayofprayer.org/news/joni-eareckson-tada/ (accessed 4 November 2011).
6. Joni Eareckson Tada, "Joni Eareckson Tada Quotes", *Christian.com,* 2011, http://www.goodreads.com/author/quotes/3715.Joni_Eareckson_Tada (accessed 20 November 2011).

TELL IT THROUGH EVANGELISM

1. Evantell, "Evantell", *Evantell,* 2010, http://evantell.org (accessed 4 November 2011).
2. Ibid.
3. Ibid.
4. Ibid.
5. Ibid.
6. Ibid.
7. Ibid.

THE GOSPEL DECLARED THROUGH SPORTS

USING HIS SECOND CHANCE

1. Jenifer Langosch, "Hamilton Finds Redemption in Faith, Sharing", *MLB.com,* 26 October 2010, http://mlb.mlb.com/news/article.jsp?ymd=20101026&content_id=15838500&vkey=news_mlb&c_id=mlb (accessed 7 November 2011).
2. Josh Hamilton with Tim Keown, *Beyond Belief: Finding the Strength to Come Back,* (New York: FaithWords, 2008).

3. Lynda Bouchard, "Josh Hamilton", *BookingAuthorsInk*, 2010, http://www.bookingauthorsink.com/client-list/83-josh-hamilton.html (accessed 21 November 2011).
4. Jenifer Langosch, "Hamilton Finds Redemption in Faith, Sharing", *MLB.com*, 26 October 2010, http://mlb.mlb.com/news/article.jsp?ymd=20101026&content_id=15838500&vkey=news_mlb&c_id=mlb (accessed 7 November 2011).
5. Wikipedia, "Josh Hamilton", *Wikipedia*, 2011, http://en.wikipedia.org/wiki/Josh_Hamilton (accessed 5 November 2011).
6. Ibid.
7. Terri Simmons, "Josh Hamilton's Fight with the Devil", *CBN 700 Club*, 2008, http://www.cbn.com/700club/guests/bios/josh_hamilton102708.aspx (accessed 7 November 2011).
8. Tim MacMahon and Richard Durrett, "Josh Hamilton addresses relapse", ESPN.com:Baseball, 2012, http://espn.go.com/espn/print?id=7537732&type=story (accessed 6 February 2012).

AN MVP FOR CHRIST

1. Emmitt Smith, "Emmitt Smith Hall of Fame Speech", *AOL News*, 8 August 2010, http://www.aolnews.com/2010/08/08/emmitt-smith-hall-of-fame-speech/ (accessed 21 November 2011).
2. Ibid.
3. Wikipedia, "Emmitt Smith", *Wikipedia*, 9 November 2011. http://en.wikipedia.org/wiki/Emmitt_Smith (accessed 21 November 2011)

THE PHOENIX OF NEW ORLEANS

1. The Brees Foundation, "Drew's Bio", *The Brees Foundation*, 2011, http://www.drewbrees.com/bio (accessed 8 November 2011).
2. Ibid.

3. Shawn Brown, "Drew Brees: The Saint of New Orleans", *CBN 700 Club*, 7 September 2010, http://www.cbn.com/700club/sports/Drew-Brees-090710.aspx (accessed 8 November 2011).
4. Ibid.

PAR EXCELLENCE FOR CHRIST

1. FCA, "About FCA", *Fellowship of Christian Athletes*, 2011, http://www.fca.org/AboutFCA/ (accessed 9 November 2011).
2. Ibid.
3. FCA, "FCA Golf", *Fellowship of Christian Athletes*, 2011, http://fcassm.org/golf (accessed 9 November 2011).
4. Clay Meyer, "Mastering the Game", *Fellowship of Christian Athletes*, 2011, http://webcache.googleusercontent.com/search?q=cache:c3-Z7_1INwgJ:www.fca.org/vsItemDisplay.lsp%3Fmethod%3Ddisplay%26objectid%3DBF767F2B-C29A-EE7A-E3430FE24128DA07+FCA+Mastering+the+Game+Zacj+Johnson&cd=11&hl=en&ct=clnk&gl=us (accessed 7 September 2011).
5. Mark Dukes, "Zach Johnson Event Over the Top", *Duke's Domain/KGYM Radio*, 2 August 2011, http://www.kgymradio.com/Zach-Johnson-event-over-the-top/7800145?archive=1&pid=57340 (accessed 21 November 2011).
6. Clay Meyer, "Mastering the Game", *Fellowship of Christian Athletes*, 2011, http://webcache.googleusercontent.com/search?q=cache:c3-Z7_1INwgJ:www.fca.org/vsItemDisplay.lsp%3Fmethod%3Ddisplay%26objectid%3DBF767F2B-C29A-EE7A-E3430FE24128DA07+FCA+Mastering+the+Game+Zacj+Johnson&cd=11&hl=en&ct=clnk&gl=us (accessed 7 September 2011).

WITNESSING WITH HIS EYES

1. Wikipedia, "Tim Tebow", *Wikipedia*, 5 June 2011, http://en.wikipedia.org/wiki/Tim_Tebow (accessed 12 November 2011.)
2. David M. Virkler, "Tim Tebow's Eye-Catching Faith", *NEWSpoint*, 1 July 2011, http://en.wikipedia.org/wiki/Tim_Tebow (accessed 10 November 2011).

THE GOSPEL EXPRESSED THROUGH MUSIC

1. "psalm", *dictionary.com*, 2011, http://dictionary.reference.com/browse/psalm (accessed 11 November 2011).

FAITH SURVIVES LIFE'S TRAGEDIES

1. Jane Winstead, "Horatio G. Spafford: The Story Behind the Hymn 'It is Well with My Soul'", *Yahoo! Contributor Network*, 29 June 2008, http://www.associatedcontent.com/article/850395/horatio_g_spafford_the_story_behind.html?cat=38 (accessed 11 November 2011).
2. Ibid.

A MUSICIAN SINCE CHILDHOOD

1. David Meece Ministries, "David Meece", *CBN Music.com*, 2011, http://www.cbn.com/cbnmusic/artists/meece_david.aspx (accessed 21 November 2011).
2. Ibid.

YOUNG CHILD, BIG VOICE FOR THE LORD

1. "Rhema Marvanne", *Rhema Marvanne.com*, 2010, http://www.rhemamarvanne.com/about.html (accessed 11 November 2011).

CHRISTIAN SONGWRITERS OF THE CENTURY

1. "Bill Gaither", *Bill Gaither News*, 2011, http://gaither.com/artists/bill-gaither (accessed 21 November 2011).
2. Debra Gordon, "The Nashville Choir Honors the Rich Musical History of Bill & Gloria Gaither", *Harmonic Progression Nashville Music Buzz*, 2 May 2011, http://nashvillemusicbuzz.wordpress.com/2011/05/02/the-nashville-choir-honors-the-rich-musical-history—of-bill-gloria-gaither/ (accessed 21 November 2011).
3. Ibid.
4. "Bill Gaither", *Bill Gaither News*, 2011, http://gaither.com/artists/bill-gaither (accessed 21 November 2011).

THE GOSPEL ADVANCED IN THE BUSINESS WORLD

CHICK-FIL-A®

1. "Company Fact Sheet", *Chick-Fil-A®*, 201,. http://www.chick-fil-a.com/Company/Highlights-Fact-Sheets (accessed 22 November 2011).
2. Wikipedia, "Chick-Fil-A", *Wikipedia*, 16 May 2011, http://en.wikipedia.org/wiki/Chick-fil-A (accessed 15 November 2011).
3. "Chick-Fil-A CEO, S. Truett Cathy", *ChristiaNet*, 2011, http://christiannews.christianet.com/1097585115.htm (accessed 14 November 2011).
4. Eric Shindelbower, "Closed on Sunday—Chick-Fil-A Restaurants®" *TheCross-Photo.com*, 2002, http://www.thecross-photo.com/Chick-fil-A_Restaurants-Closed_On_Sunday.htm (accessed 12 November 2011).

HOBBY LOBBY

1. Mark Martin, "The Secret to David Green's Successful "Hobby", *CBN News*, 21 January 2011, http://www.cbn.com/cbnnews/

finance/2010/November/The-Secret-to-David-Greens-Successful-Hobby/ (accessed 15 November 2011).
2. "Hobby Lobby CEO, David Green", *ChristiaNet*, 1996-2011, http://christiannews.christianet.com/1096289115.htm (accessed 15 November 2011).
3. Ibid.
4. Mark Martin, "The Secret to David Green's Successful "Hobby", *CBN News*, 21 January 2011, http://www.cbn.com/cbnnews/finance/2010/November/The-Secret-to-David-Greens Successful-Hobby/ (accessed 15 November 2011).
5. Geraldine Fabrikant, "Craft Shop Family Busy Up Ancient Bibles for Museum", *The New York Times Business Day*, 11 June 2010, http://www.nytimes.com/2010/06/12/business/12bibles.html?pagewanted=all (accessed 15 November 2011.

MARDEL CHRISTIAN STORES
1. American Eagle.com, Inc., "Mardel Christian & Education", *About Us*, 2011, http://www.mardel.com/about/ (accessed 15 November 2011).
2. Mart Green, "Mart Green This Book is Alive™", Mart Green, 2008, http://www.martgreen.net/ (accessed 5 November 2011).
3. American Eagle.com, Inc., "Mardel Christian & Education", *About Us: Mission Statement*, 2011, http://www.mardel.com/about/mission.aspx (accessed 15 November 2011).
4. Ibid.
5. Wikipedia, "Mart Green", *Wikipedia*, 17 July 2011, http://en.wikipedia.org/wiki/Mart_Green (accessed 15 November 2011).

INTERSTATE BATTERY SYSTEM OF AMERICA

1. "Norm Miller: Personal Testimony", *Interstate Battery System International, Inc.*, 2011, http://corporate.interstatebatteries.com/norm_miller/testimony/ (accessed 15 November 2011).
2. "Mission Philosophy", *Interstate Battery System International, Inc.*, 2011, http://corporate.interstatebatteries.com/mission/ (accessed 15 November 2011).

JM EAGLE COMPANY

1. Mark Martin, "Businessman Pipes 'Living Water" to the World, *Christian Broadcasting Network*, 6 January 2011, http://www.cbn.com/cbnnews/us/2010/July/Businessman-Pipes-Living-Water-to-the-World/ (accessed 15 November 2011).
2. Ibid.
3. Ibid.
4. Ibid.

A MISSION ON THE AIRWAVES

1. "About CBN, Mission and History of CBN", *CBN.com*, 2011, http://www.cbn.com/about/index.aspx?WT.svl=menu (accessed 20 May 2011).
2. Ibid.
3. "CBN's Mission Statement", *CBN.com*, 2011, http://www.cbn.com/about/mission/Mission_Statement.aspx (accessed 20 May 2011).

THE TEA LADY

1. Eileen Hadaway, "The Key to Her Business Success" *CBN.com*, The 700 Club, 8 June 2011, http://www.cbn.com/media/player/index.aspx?s=/mp4/LEAD323v5_WS (accessed 14 December 2011).

HOLY LAND EXPERIENCE

1. "History", *The Holy Land Experience,* 2011, http://www.holyland experience.com/about/history.html (accessed 14 December 2011).

DAYSPRING CARDS

1. "About DaySpring, History", *DaySpring,* 2011, http://about.dayspring.com (accessed 16 November 2011).
2. "About DaySpring, Our Mission Statement", *DaySpring,* 2011, http://about.dayspring.com/corporate/mission.asp (accessed 16 November 2011).
3. "About DaySpring, Ministry Outreach", *DaySpring,* 2011, http://about.dayspring.com/corporate/outreach.asp (accessed 16 November 2011).

MARKETPLACE CHAPLAINS

1. "A Brief Ministry History", *Marketplace Ministries,* 2011, http://www.marketplaceministries.com/AboutUs-Overview.aspx (accessed 18 November, 2011).
2. "Web Exclusive: Marketplace Chaplains USA" *Marketplace Ministries,* 2011, http://www.dfwchristianfamily.com/missionsAndMinistry/Marketplace-Chaplains-USA.php (accessed 17 November 2011).
3. "About Us", *Marketplace Ministries,* 2011, http://mchapusa.com/about-us (accessed 18 November 2011).

GOD'S OTHER WAYS

POW SUSTAINED BY GOD'S POWER

1. Sam Johnson and Jan Winebrenner, *Captive Warriors A Vietnam POW's Story.* (College Station: Texas A & M University Press, 1992), 46.
2. Ibid., 184.

3. Ibid., 247.
4. Ibid., 247.
5. Ibid., 188.

SHE SAVED SIX YEARS TO BUY A BIBLE
1. Bible Society, "Mary Jones", *Bible Society*, 2011, http://www.biblesociety.org.uk/about-bible-society/history/mary-jones/ (accessed 17 November 2011).
2. Bible Society, "Why We Exist," *Bible Society*, 2011, http://www.biblesociety.org.uk/about-bible-society/why-we-exist/ (accessed 17 November 2011).
3. Bible Society, "Mary Jones", *Bible Society*, 2011, http://www.biblesociety.org.uk/about-bible-society/history/mary-jones/ (accessed 17 November 2011).
4. Ibid.

MY HERO
1. Anonymous, "One Solitary Life", *Anna Lucci*, 2011, http://www.annalucci.com/files/OneSolitaryLife-star.pdf (accessed 17 November 2011).

WARNED TO ESCAPE FROM HIROSHIMA
1. Douglas Connelly, "Angels Around Us: What the Bible Really Says", (Downers Grove: InterVarsity Press, 1994).
2. Ibid., 131.
3. Ibid., 132.

SEIZE ANY CHANCE TO PRAY
1. Cain, Jerry. "Re: Ken Kersey's short stories". Message to Kenneth R. Kersey. 25 August 2010. E-mail.

PLANT HIS WORD, HE WILL GROW IT
1. "Meet Charles Swindoll", *Christianbook.com*, 2003, http://www.christianbook.com/html/authors/83.html (accessed 9 June 2011).
2. "God's Word—It Never Returns Void", *Insight for Living*, 4 May 2011, http://insightforliving.typepad.com/insight_for_living_blog/2011/05/gods-word-it-never-returns-void.html (accessed 23 November 2011).

TRIALS STRENGTHEN HER FAITH
1. Young, Kay. "Re: Friends—Need your help!". Message to Kenneth R. Kersey. 18 September 2010. E-mail.

GOD IS SOVEREIGN
1. Dubert, Marjorie. "Re: Your request". Message to Kenneth R. Kersey. 5 September 2010. E-mail.

GOD USES WEATHER AND NATURE
1. Lee Paul, "Noah's Ark", *The Unexplained*, October 10, 2011, http://www.theoutlaws.com/unexplained9.htm (accessed 27 November 2011).
2. "The Flood Tablet, relating part of the Epic of Gilgamesh", *The British Museum*, 2011, http://www.britishmuseum.org/explore/highlights/highlight_objects/me/t/the_flood_tablet.as px (accessed 27 November 2011).
3. Peter Marshall and David Manuel, "The Light and the Glory", Old Tappan: Fleming H. Revell Company, 1940), 31.
4. "Christopher Columbus Biography Page 3", *123Holiday.net*, 2011, http://columbus-day.123holiday.net/christopher_columbus_3.html (accessed 27 November 2011).

5. Evelyn Dole, "A tornado that saved a city and defeated the enemy", *Air Force Print News,* March 6, 2007, http://www.afweather.af.mil/news/story.asp?id=123042444 (accessed 27 November 2011).
6. Jennifer Terhune, "The Battle of New Orleans", *Jen's Pen,* 21 January 2010, http://www.jenspen.com/2010/01/battle-of-new-orleans.html (accessed 23 November 2011).
7. Douglas S. Winnail, "The Weather Factor!", *Tomorrow's World,* 2011, http://www.tomorrowsworld.org/magazines/2004/nov-dec/the-weather-factor (accessed 26 November 2011).
8. Ibid.

WORDLESS BOOK AND BRACELETS

1. Wikipedia, "Wordless Book", *Wikipedia,* 2011. http://en.wikipedia.org/wiki/Wordless_Book (accessed 24 May 2011).
2. "The Wordless Book, "*Squidoo, LLC,* 2011, http://www.squidoo.com/the-wordless-book (accessed 24 May 2011).
3. "Salvation Bracelets", *Jeff Goss Ministries,* 2006-2011, http://jeffgossministries.org/salvationbracelets.asp (accessed 24 May 2011).

"PERMIT THE CHILDREN TO COME TO ME"

1. "CEF Child Evangelism Fellowship About Us", *Child Evangelism Fellowship,* 2010, http://www.cefonline.com/index.php?option=com_content&view=section&id=8&Itemid=100032 (accessed 24 November 2011).

POLIO MAKES THERAPY HER LIFE'S WORK

1. McKinley, Donna. "Re: Attn: Donna McKinley—Need your help!". Message to Kenneth R. Kersey. 20 June 2010. E-mail.

PARACHUTING THE GOSPEL

1. "About VOM", *The Voice of the Martyrs*, 2011, https://persecution.com/public/aboutVOM.aspx?clickfrom=bWFpbl9tZW51 (accessed 25 November 2011).
2. "American Christians Help Spread Gospel to FARC Guerillas", *Voice of the Martyrs*, 2011, http://www.persecution.com/parachute (accessed 25 November 2011).
3. Jonathan J. Bonk, "Mission by the Numbers", *International Bulletin of Missionary Research*, January, 2011, http://www.internationalbulletin.org/files/html/2011-01-home.html (accessed 25 November 2011).
4. Ibid.
5. "Christian Martyrs—Not Just Ancient History", *Creative Ministry Trend Analysis Report*, 2003, http://www.creativeministry.org/article.php?id=969&action=print (accessed 25 November 2011).
6. "FAQs", The *Voice of the Martyrs*, 2011, http://www.persecution.net/faq.htm (accessed 25 November 2011).

SHE MET GOD "IN THE GARDEN"

1. Sims, Jeanelle. "Re: My Testimony". Message to Kenneth R. Kersey. 1 July 2010. E-mail.
2. "In the Garden", *Christian Counseling & Educational Services*, 2011. http://www.ccesonline.com/hymns/inthegarden.htm (accessed 24 November 2011).

MINERS SAVED HALF MILE UNDERGROUND

1. Kayla Webley, "How the Chilean Miners Survived the First 17 Days", *Time*, 24 August 2010, http://www.time.com/time/magazine/article/0,9171,2017215,00.html (accessed 14 December 2011).
2. Trevor Persaud, "Chilean Miner: 'God Has Never Left Us'". *ChristianityToday live blog*, 12 October 2010, http://blog.

christianitytoday.com/ctliveblog/archives/2010/10/chilean_miner_g.html (accessed 24 November 2011).

3. Ibid.

4. Staff Writer, The *JESUS* Film Project, "*Help Give 'Jesus' to Everyone, Everywhere . . . And Change Lives for Eternity*," 2011, http://www.jesusfilm.org/ (accessed 24 November 2011).

TRUST HIM, GOD KNOWS BEST

1. Kersey, Joe, "Re: Family—Book". Message to Kenneth R. Kersey. 25 July 2010. E-mail.

LOSS TURNS TO GAIN

1. Dinovo, Frank, "Re: Need your help!". Message to Kenneth R. Kersey. 15 Jun 2010. E-mail.

SILENT WITNESS—THE GROUND ZERO CROSS

1. Frank Silecchia, "The Cross at Ground Zero". Guideposts, 25 August 2011, http://www.guideposts.org/faith-and-hope/faith-renewed-cross-ground-zero (accessed 6 February 2012).

2. Wikipedia, "World Trade Center cross", *Wikipedia*, 22 November 2011, http://en.wikipedia.org/wiki/World_Trade_Center_cross (accessed 25 November 2011).

3. Ibid.

AS IT WAS IN THE DAYS OF NOAH . . .

1. Anugrah Kumar, Christian Post Reporter, "Life-Size Noah's Ark Replica Open in Hong Kong". *The Chistian Post,* 19 July 2011, http://sg.christianpost.com/dbase/asia/917/section/1.htm (accessed 25 November 2011).

2. Ibid.

3. Katherine T. Phan, Christian Post Reporter, "Noah's Ark Theme Park Attraction in Ky. Raises $3 Million", *The Christian Post*, 31 May, 2011, http://www.christianpost.com/news/biblical-theme—park-in-ky-raises-3-million-toward-noahs-ark-attraction-50695/ (accessed 25 November 2011).
4. Associated Press, "Noah's Ark Replica Being Built in Kentucky", *Fox News.com*, 02 October 2011, http://www.foxnews.com/travel/2011/10/02/noahs-ark-replica-being-built-in-kentucky/ (accessed 25 November 2011).
5. Laurie Goodstein, "In Kentucky, Noah's Ark Theme Park is Planned", *New York Times*, 5 December 2010, http://www.nytimes.com/2010/12/06/us/06ark.html (accessed 25 November 2011).
6. Chris Mitchell, "Life-Size Ark Replica Takes Shape in Holland", *CBN News*, 28 August 2011, http://www.cbn.com/cbnnews/world/2011/August/Life-Size-Ark-Replica-Takes-Shape-in-Holland-/ (accessed 25 November 2011).
7. Ibid.
8. Allan Hall, "Now that's what I call an Olympic event: Life-sized replica of Noah's Ark to sail up Thames for 2012, Games complete with animals", *Daily Mail*, 1 June 2011, www.dailymail.co.uk/news/article-1392775/London-2012-Olympics-Life-size-Noahs-Ark-sail-Thames.html (accessed 25 November 2011).

THE END

1. Josh McDowell, "Josh McDowell Quotes", *Christian.com*, 1999-2010, http://christian-quotes.ochristian.com/Josh-McDowell-Quotes/ (accessed 27 November 2011).

CPSIA information can be obtained at www.ICGtesting.com
Printed in the USA
LVOW061152220612
287245LV00002B/4/P